Fragments

GOD'S PATTERN IN
LIFE'S PIECES

DAN WOLGEMUTH

YOUTHFORCHRIST

© Youth for Christ, 2010

Published by Youth for Christ/USA
7670 S. Vaughn Ct.
Englewood, CO 80112
www.yfc.net

Printed in the United States of America

ISBN : 978-0-9724616-5-8

Produced with the assistance of The Livingstone Corporation (www.LivingstoneCorp.com). Project staff includes Bruce Barton, Dave Veerman, Linda Taylor, Linda Washington, Ashley Taylor, Dan van Loon. Cover and interior designed by Larry Taylor.

In honor of Grace Wolgemuth and Don Cargo, my mother and father-in-law.
Inspirations in life . . . warriors in dying . . . and now citizens of Glory.
Your dignity, joy, and laughter still ring in our hearts.
You lived in praise of our God.

It has been said that your world is only different by
"the people you meet and the books you read. . . ."
I have met Dan and now I have read his book—and my world is different.

D. J. BUHLER

INTRODUCTION

APRIL 1, 2005 WAS a Friday. It was also my first day as the National President of Youth for Christ/USA.

I remember it distinctly. I spent the first day on the job in my home in Lenexa, Kansas, a location where Mary and I had lived for almost twelve years. Our official journey to Denver wouldn't take place until Sunday, but I was "on the clock" on Friday. I had been "on the clock" for twenty-eight years in a variety of business contexts. YFC was officially my seventh career move, but it felt like unfamiliar territory. I woke on Friday morning to the fresh reminders of this reality. God had patiently and unavoidably drawn me into the ministry of Youth for Christ/USA. For many years I had been a volunteer, a vantage point that confirmed the significance of the ministry as well as illuminated the challenges of such a step.

On my first Friday morning with YFC, I spent time reading, thinking, anticipating and praying. My collection of professional experience and my personal journey with Christ seemed to flood light on this pathway in my life; and yet I felt overwhelmed and underequipped.

And so I sat at a keyboard and wrote. It was a prayer I wrote—a paraphrase of the Lord's Prayer. I wrote it to the YFC/USA community. To friends and to strangers. As my fingers moved across the letters in front of me, it was as though I connected to the very people I was writing to. Within a couple of hours June Thompson, my very capable assistant, had electronically distributed the document throughout the YFC network . . . and with that a Friday email was launched.

In a week or two we had officially named it "The Friday Fragment," and shortly after that the prayers morphed into a more introspective and reflective theme. And it was this transformation that escorted me to a place of heightened sensitivity to the unique and personal ways that our heavenly Father illuminates and connects the disconnected and isolated moments and experiences in our lives. It was this reality that drew me to the theme, and far more importantly, to God and to His master plan for life and living.

I also love the metaphor of fragments when it comes to the mission of Youth for Christ. Young lives are broken and disconnected as never before. Many of the functional and relational issues that used to characterize third world countries are now reflected in urban and rural communities in North America. As we discover God's pattern and His plan through the pieces of our lives, we will understand the richness of His love and the power of His transformation. The mortar and cement that connect these broken pieces are nothing short of the power of God. And as we discover, embrace and rely on this power, we will see transformation and celebration. This is why and what inspires me to write.

A fragment.

Just a piece . . . a small component of the whole. A splinter off an entire board. A journal entry without a history.

"I know in part; then . . . someday, in ways too powerful and beautiful for words, I will know fully."

The apostle Paul's words explode across the page. Yes, today we know only in Fragments . . . 400-word sound bites that expose only one piece of the breathtaking mosaic, only one brush stroke of the masterpiece, only one measure of a brilliant symphony, only one pixel in the heart-stopping picture, only one color in the sunset.

That's why . . . Fragments. It's all I know. It's all I can comprehend. It's all my mind can contain. But it is why I write. It is why one entry is about my personal struggles, another expresses my complete joy, and still others plumb the depths of family pain . . . it's just a part, my one-week thread in the tapestry of life.

But make no mistake . . . fragments fit. God the Father takes ownership of the context that provides the perfect place for every piece to slip appropriately into.

God makes a flawless quilt out of the patches of our lives. We see only isolation; He, and He alone, sees the symmetry and majesty of the whole.

Now in part . . . but someday I will know fully as the light of eternity bursts through the beautiful collection of pieces that have been masterfully and sovereignly placed together to create what I could never have conceived. But until then . . . Fragments.

CONTENTS

·CONTENTS·

· CONTENTS ·

·CONTENTS·

FRAGMENTS

Fragments

THE GIFT OF GRACE

For by grace you have been saved through faith. And this is not your own doing; it is the gift of God, not a result of works, so that no one may boast.

(EPHESIANS 2:8, 9)

I HAD CLICKED THROUGH all of the appropriate and necessary screens, and now I was on the final confirmation page. The expected costs were illuminated, the credit card information entered, and then one final question.

While I don't remember the wording of the question verbatim, I do remember the gist. "If you would like to upgrade to elite status for this flight, indicate here."

I don't remember exactly the cost for this upgrade . . . $25 or $35 I think, but what I do remember is how it made me react.

Elite Status was designed to be a specific grace dispensed for travelers who, out of loyalty and patronage, had been bestowed with the privileges granted by a grateful airline. Now, for a nominal fee, you can purchase this status, you can buy this favor, you can replace loyalty with cash.

As I stared into the screen on my laptop, I was struck by the implications of this reality and appalled at the revelation that it exposed.

Loyalty has a cycle of maturity that simply takes too long. In the mind of the dispenser, a grace given for commitment demonstrated can now become a profit center. Status is no longer granted; it's purchased. Appreciation can be bought.

No longer are the individuals at the front of the line at the airport gate those who are road weary and security-line tested. The individuals at the front may have cut in line to get there—or rather paid an additional fee to get there.

And besides all of that, this practice now cheapens the grace that used to be a reflection of a grateful vendor.

Frankly, it changes everything about the status, the experience, and the intended consequences of the program.

God has us figured out. He knows that grace that can be bought or earned produces a very different result in our heart and mind.

By grace . . . so I said no to the upgrade. No up-charge on my credit card. Grace is a gift; grace is mercy.

Thanks be to God for his inexpressible gift!

(2 CORINTHIANS 9:15)

He saved us, not because of works done by us in righteousness,
but according to his own mercy.

(TITUS 3:5)

Our status is impossible for us to purchase, but it is secure in the hands of our Savior.

SURROUNDED

Therefore, since we are surrounded by so great a cloud of witnesses, let us also lay aside every weight, and sin which clings so closely, and let us run with endurance the race that is set before us, looking to Jesus, the founder and perfecter of our faith, who for the joy that was set before him endured the cross, despising the shame, and is seated at the right hand of the throne of God.

(HEBREWS 12:1, 2)

THE 2008 LEADVILLE 100 was a painful disappointment to Lance Armstrong, the world-famous cyclist. While Lance has never been known for his prowess on a mountain bike—the type of bike needed for this race—he certainly is known as someone who hates to lose. And lose he did, to the forty-three-year-old reigning champion. The grueling one hundred miles through the mountains surrounding Leadville, Colorado, create an unforgiving and pain-filled marathon. Some contend that it was this loss that propelled Lance back into the pro-cycling circuit.

So on August 15, 2009, on a cold, wet, and painfully uninviting morning, riders raced from the start at 6:30 a.m. While this was no Tour de France (which Lance had completed a month before), it was a personal grudge match for Lance. He intended to win the 2009 Leadville 100.

Through nearly all of the first half of the race, Lance relied on the steady and sacrificial support of his partners—his buddies, his teammates. In large part, it was Matt Shriver who led the way. He set a blistering pace at his own expense that led to the early demise of many serious competitors. He carved the way, with Lance tucked right in behind him.

Then, with the will and fortitude of others failing, Lance was ready. Shriver had been his cover, his windshield, his pacesetter . . . and now the timing was right for Lance to make his move.

And move he did. As though it was an Indianapolis race car against a showroom Ford. He disappeared.

Avenge he did. Beating the 2008 champion by over thirty minutes. But when Lance crossed the finish line after nearly six hours and thirty minutes, he did so with a flat tire. In fact, he had ridden on the underinflated rear tire for nearly ten miles. He had stopped and re-inflated it several times, but without lasting success.

When asked about the race and the condition of his back tire when he finished, Lance gave the appropriate credit and made the honest confession. He certainly knew that Matt Shriver had helped him accomplish his goal. He had sacrificed himself for his companion. And about the flat tire . . . Armstrong admitted that although he has traveled thousands and thousands of miles on a bicycle, he really doesn't know how to change a tire.

In nearly every other situation, Lance is surrounded by those who are committed to helping him complete his race. He has dedicated teams that have both equipment and expertise to help him compete and complete his course. At the end of the Leadville 100, Lance was alone. He had no answer to the problem of his flat tire. Without his team, he was at a distinct disadvantage.

As the writer to the Hebrews described, it is beautiful to be surrounded. When the tire is flat. When the oxygen is thin. When the mountains loom. When the pain and emptiness persist.

Setting the pace and fixing the flats . . . oh, how I've needed my companions.

Jesus, the founder and perfecter of our faith, died on the cross so that I'm never alone on the race that is set before me. He is with me every step of the way; my buddies, my friends, my fellow believers are supporting, praying, helping. And that great cloud of witnesses? They are cheering me on!

FORM AND FUNCTION

Blessed are the poor in spirit, for theirs is the kingdom of heaven. Blessed are those who mourn, for they shall be comforted. Blessed are the meek, for they shall inherit the earth. Blessed are those who hunger and thirst for righteousness, for they shall be satisfied.

(MATTHEW 5:3-6)

FOR SEVERAL YEARS I frequented the Tower Thistle Hotel in London. The property is situated on the Thames River beside the Tower Bridge. The proximity of the hotel made it very convenient for regular business meetings. Without exception I found myself spellbound as I walked into the hotel. The elegance and beauty of the bridge captured me, regardless of the weightiness of the business agenda.

The uniqueness of the Tower Bridge is best defined as the perfection of form and function coming together. The breathtaking visual appeal provides a compelling invitation to come, while the engineering, the stone, and the steel provide a worthy platform for use. This is not a static landmark but rather a dynamic, heavily utilized transportation corridor.

This complete picture—the power of form and function dancing in complimentary harmony—provides a snapshot of the syllabus that I believe Jesus was using in His teaching in the Sermon on the Mount. The very first words of His discourse in Matthew 5:3-11 center on the finesse that exists between beauty and power. Strength and comfort come together to provide a bond that Christians are wise to understand.

Humility, mercy, brokenness, and peacemaking embrace righteousness, holiness, courage and zeal. It is a beautiful, invitational message that accommodates the rush-hour traffic of real life. To miss the balance is to shortcut the message. Too much "form" and we provide the "appearance of godliness, but denying its power" (2 Timothy 3:5). Too much function and we provide a thoroughfare without traffic. "The love of Christ controls us. . . . Therefore, we are ambassadors for Christ, God making his appeal through us" (2 Corinthians 5:14, 20).

The authentic message of Jesus is attractive, just as it is strong and sure.

Legalism and liberalism are not in the design of this bridge. It is engineered by the love of God and constructed with the sacrificial steel of Jesus' blood. Yes, form and function dance together. They provide a beautiful pathway that will stand against all enemies. It is a narrow pathway, but it is sure and lined with hope.

This is the substance of what Jonathan Edwards called the "diverse excellencies" of God. It is rich, beautiful, *and* useful. It invites as it accomplishes.

Truth with compassion. Love without compromise.

Form embracing function. A bridge of beauty that sustains the traffic.

TRUTH WHERE YOU LIVE

The word of God is living and active, sharper than any two-edged sword,
piercing to the division of soul and of spirit, of joints and of marrow, and discerning
the thoughts and intentions of the heart.

(HEBREWS 4:12)

ON A TUESDAY I took Mary to the airport for a nineteen-day journey to Europe. After an overnight flight, she connected with our daughter, Alli, at Heathrow Airport in London, at the conclusion of Alli's twelve-week semester of college study in Tanzania.

Once I returned to our house, I began my bachelor experience. At 10:30 p.m., when I pulled back the covers of our bed, I found a card from Mary taped to the sheet. It was expertly crafted by hand, and expressed in tender terms the love and commitment that she has for me. It was ointment on a lonely heart.

The next morning it was time to make a smaller than usual pot of coffee, and as I reached for the filters inside a kitchen cabinet, I found a note taped to the box. A reminder of Mary's love once again. Her own words—her own hands—confirmed what I believed.

Over the next three days, it was like an Easter egg hunt. Except I was not hunting at all. Messages of love, commitment, support, and care showed up in the spots where I live. Taped to the bottom of a remote control. Perfectly placed in the center of the seat I typically occupy at the kitchen table. On top of the second pair of underwear in my closet. On the register page of the checkbook. On the shower door. On a plate of leftover calzones that we had originally shared the previous Sunday.

Right where I live—reminders, reflections, and words of renewal.

Mary could have typed all of the words, put them on a page or two and dropped them on the kitchen counter. But she knew that the words would impact me more directly when I experienced them where I live. And so I left them as close to where I found them as possible, because they came alive in context; and I basked in what they communicated, every time I saw them.

The author of the book of Hebrews understood this. Under the inspiration of the Holy Spirit these words were written: "The word of God is living and active, sharper than any two-edged sword, piercing to the division of soul and of spirit, of joints and of marrow, and discerning the thoughts and intentions of the heart" (Hebrews 4:12). Because the Word of God lives where we live. It applies to what we experience. It moves what we can't budge. It assures when and where we doubt. It embraces where we feel alone. It convicts when we disobey. God's Word is where we are. His truth lives in our reality. Inspired at its creation, applied in real-time by His Spirit.

I'm loved and cared for . . . at every turn, in every way.

IN THE GARDEN

For the LORD comforts Zion; he comforts all her waste places and makes her wilderness like Eden, her desert like the garden of the Lord; joy and gladness will be found in her, thanksgiving and the voice of song.

(ISAIAH 51:3)

ONE TUESDAY NIGHT I stayed at the home of Larry and Robin Becker, ministry partners from Indianapolis. They hosted a reception in their home and extended a welcome to me. Just pulling into the Beckers' home was a treat. Their property was a picture of what spring should look like. The lawn, the trees, the flowers, the placement of every rock is precise but inviting, exploding with life and color and richness.

Larry and Robin's house is an advertisement for the business they've grown in central Indiana. Becker Landscape has been around since Larry walked behind a lawn mower as a middle school student. Larry knows the business and he knows the trade. His home reflects every aspect of his commitment to excellence and quality.

That Tuesday afternoon I got a glimpse of what the garden of Eden might have looked like. I smelled and saw the power of that beauty. God went to extraordinary lengths to create this wonder.

Unfortunately, I don't live in the garden. Like Adam and Eve, I opted out. I felt entitled to more. I wanted control. It's hard to imagine, but it's true.

Therefore the LORD God sent him out from the garden of Eden to work the ground from which he was taken. He drove out the man, and at the east of the garden of Eden he placed the cherubim and a flaming sword that turned every way to guard the way to the tree of life.

(GENESIS 3:23, 24)

So for now, I live in the wilderness. A place east of the garden. A place of struggle, of disease, of disappointment, of greed, of selfishness, and of death.

But every once in a while . . . just to remind me . . . God gives me a glimpse of Eden. Flashing across the barrenness of the desert I spot an oasis, a snapshot of what was and what will be.

Every once in a while—sometimes in the face of a friend, sometimes in the act of a perfect stranger, sometimes in the sacrifice of a partner, sometimes in the service of a disciple, sometimes in the generosity of a colleague, sometimes in the laughter of a child, yes, and sometimes in the front yard of the Beckers—I get a glimpse of Eden, a snapshot of what God intended and a vision of what will be.

We were made for that garden. Being with the Beckers reminded me.

POINTS
OF WEAKNESS

Search me, O God, and know my heart! Try me and know my thoughts! And see if
there be any grievous way in me, and lead me in the way everlasting!

(PSALM 139:23, 24)

THE VERDICT HASN'T BEEN completely established at this point, but it seems that some combination of weight and weakness proved lethal in downtown Minneapolis. The bridge over the Mississippi River fractured when a point of failure and vulnerability was exposed.

Undoubtedly it will take months to determine the exact cause, but each day more speculation exists that the combination of construction equipment weight and growing weaknesses in the bridge collided. The result created a cascade of disaster that rippled through the entire river span. Even areas of strength crumbled when points of dependency failed in catastrophic proportion. Cars, buses and trucks were tossed from the bridge as those that trusted the infrastructure were impacted by the breach.

The scenario is all too familiar. The lethal combination is much too frequently repeated. Weight and weakness collide, an infrastructure collapses and lives, families, children, organizations, neighborhoods are tossed into chaos.

A flaw is exposed before it is dealt with; the pressure and opportunity of everyday life press into the crack and disaster is the result.

God understands the need for inspection. He loves us enough to want full disclosure before we experience full disaster.

When weakness intersects with the weight of everyday living, innocent people are flung from the bridge. Unsuspecting individuals are caught in the chaos. Disaster.

Is it time to double check the spans in your life? The disaster metaphor is much too poignant to miss. Yes, dear Lord, "search me," expose the points of weakness. Relieve the stress points. Then lead me. I trust You. I need You.

13

WHAT THE
FATHER WILLS

Come now, you who say, "Today or tomorrow we will go into such and such a town
and spend a year there and trade and make a profit"— yet you do not know what
tomorrow will bring. What is your life? For you are a mist that appears for a little time
and then vanishes. Instead you ought to say, "If the Lord wills, we will live and do this
or that." As it is, you boast in your arrogance. All such boasting is evil. So whoever
knows the right thing to do and fails to do it, for him it is sin.

(JAMES 4:13-17)

MIRAGE STORAGE. THIS STATEMENT is shown at the top of a
small billboard that sits on a corner lot about one hundred yards from
my office. I've driven past it many, many times. Frankly, it wasn't until
a morning in the fall of 2008 that I actually read what it said. I've seen
the artist's rendering of what the commercial building would look like,
but I haven't paid attention to the promise made at the top.

For the sake of clarity, you should know that this lot remains vacant
two years later. Weeds are cropped to an acceptable but not attractive level. Part of the grand irony is the name of the building . . . yes, a
mirage indeed. Perhaps the joke is on me.

And yet this morning, the impact was far greater than simply a play
on words. I was drawn to the times when I've posted similar signs in
my life.

Coming Soon.

Really? Can I absolutely predict the future? Do I know what the
economy will do? What the doctor will say? What the weather will
bring? Can I guarantee what others will say or how they will react?

Plans are good. Even renderings of what we think the future might look like. But for Christians there needs to always be an echo in the bottom of our soul that says, "If the Lord wills." There isn't anything magic about saying it, but there is something vital about acknowledging that our Father, the God of the universe, is ultimately in control. His will trumps our plans. He knows what I can't ever perceive.

Planning without humility is an offense to the Creator.

"If the Lord wills" is not an excuse for laziness or sloppiness; rather, it's an invitation into the splendor of His sovereign design. It's a place where hard work and rest can coexist. A place for sweat without worry, for confidence without arrogance.

Coming Soon.

What the Father wills . . . build there.

A PERFECT SCORE

For our sake he made him to be sin who knew no sin, so that in him
we might become the righteousness of God.

(2 CORINTHIANS 5:21)

MY SCORE WAS A sixty-four and I was elated. On a beautiful Monday afternoon, I played golf as part of the Denver Youth for Christ annual outing. The course was perfectly manicured and equally challenging.

What made the day, and more specifically, the score of eight under par possible, was the foursome that I was a part of. Brad is a YFC staffer and a great golfer. Kelly is a businessman and YFC Board member. Even with a very sore back, he had a short game to be envied. And Roger Cross, past President of YFC and my dear friend, did his part as well.

Because of the tournament format and scoring, these wonderful players became my partners. Their swing was my swing. Their outstanding drives, their skilled chip shots, and their accurate putts were mine. For example, after four holes we had yet to use any of my shots; yet, my scorecard read four under par! My total reflected the talent of Brad, Kelly and Roger.

When the goodness and loving kindness of God our Savior appeared, he saved us, not
because of works done by us in righteousness, but according to his own mercy.

(TITUS 3:4, 5)

The apostle Paul understood this concept at a radically personal and eternal level. He understood that no swing he could take in his spiritual life could attain the objective or standard of God. So, enter mercy: Christ's strokes on my scorecard.

Every drive, every chip, every putt is the Savior's; sixty-four becomes my total!

Jesus: His swing, His expertise, His righteousness . . . my score. What sacrifice, what love.

BEAUTIFUL BRIDE

Then I heard what seemed to be the voice of a great multitude, like the roar of many waters and like the sound of mighty peals of thunder, crying out, "Hallelujah! For the Lord our God the Almighty reigns. Let us rejoice and exult and give him the glory, for the marriage of the Lamb has come, and his Bride has made herself ready; it was granted her to clothe herself with fine linen, bright and pure"— for the fine linen is the righteous deeds of the saints.

(Revelation 19:6-8)

IT WAS A RESTAURANT in the Cherry Creek shopping area of Denver. A trendy Italian menu and ambiance provided the perfect backdrop for an anniversary dinner celebrating thirty-one years of marriage.

The table we were allocated was perfect. The wait staff found that special balance of attentiveness and privacy, and our evening evaporated into conversation, reflection, and thanksgiving. A bright red Moleskine provided the canvas on which Mary logged the highlights of another year of experiences. Some expected, some wondrously concealed, some uninvited and difficult. But all of them experienced together.

Mary looked beautiful. More elegant. More mysterious. More profound and rich than the day I gazed down a church aisle at her in Franklin, Michigan.

From laughter to tears our reflections chased our emotions. We were surrounded but alone.

We marveled at the journey. The depths, the heights, charted and uncharted.

I loved her then . . . but never more than now.

And in that moment, that precious moment, I thought about the fact that we—you and I—are the bride of Christ. His Church, the body of believers. I reflected on the depth and beauty of His love for me, for us. Then, in that moment, I gazed into the eyes of my love and I thought for a powerful, undivided moment, about how beautiful my wife was. I thought about how proud I was to have Mary as my wife. She had honored me with her fidelity, her tenderness, her discipline, her preparation, her selflessness, and her appetite for more.

I want to be that kind of bride.

Devoted. Enthralled. Captured to the core. Inquisitive. Moved.

This is what Jesus had in mind for husbands and wives as a trailer for the full-length movie, a preview of the beauty of our life with Christ.

He is our bridegroom. Provider. Protector. Advocate. Companion. His Church. His bride.

Another year. More beautiful, more committed, more prepared, more tender, more trusting.

I got a glimpse of the bride that we should be.

ROOTED IN THE SCRIPTURES

Jesus increased in wisdom and in stature and in favor with God and man.

(LUKE 2:52)

I WOULD GUESS THAT in households across America, the holiday season always gives ample time for some healthy, and perhaps redundant, reminiscing about events of significance, entertainment, and enjoyment in the life of the family. That was usually the case in our household. In fact, the sharing tended to erupt like popcorn on a perfectly heated stove. The memories ran deep and the impact was rich. Regardless of the age of the participants, bridges were built to a legacy of God's faithfulness and care, even when the waters beneath were troubled or pain filled.

As I reflected on the power of a reflective family, I was drawn to speculation about the early days in the life of Jesus. It appears that the Gospel authors leave gaping holes in His childhood development. We're told in Matthew 2 that Joseph and Mary took their young son from Egypt back to Nazareth, but the story languishes in written account until we read about a twelve-year-old Jesus in Jerusalem for an annual family pilgrimage (Luke 2:41-52). Once this story is recounted, we again encounter more silence.

What happened in these non-descript times in the life of the Son of God? Were the first thirty years of Jesus' life so completely uneventful that they deserved no account?

Actually, the Gospel accounts do fling open a window on the early life of Jesus. We get this glimpse through subtle but powerful insights as He forms His ministry life.

At the start of the ministry of Jesus, in His earliest recorded conversations, we see what He's been doing for thirty years. It is here that the words of Jesus explode with Old Testament strength. Exodus, Leviticus, Deuteronomy, Isaiah all provided a launch pad for the initial Gospel dialogs in Jesus' ministry discourses.

Jesus had listened as a young boy sitting around the family dinner table. He had heard the prophetic words of the Old Testament authors. And at some point, maybe when He caught His mother's eye across the table, He began to know. Soon His soul confirmed what His mind was processing: It's Me. I am the one.

The Scriptures are virtually silent about the first thirty years of Jesus' life, but the explosion that occurred at age thirty fully exposes what had been happening. A family, deeply rooted in Scripture, had taken Jesus to a place where He was ready to live out the purposes of God. Building bridges indeed. To the past. To the memories. To the future.

A boy no longer . . . Jesus was ready because He'd been nurtured and taught in the ways of God. May we learn the lessons of Nazareth between the manger and the ministry. Bathed in the richness of Scripture from His earliest memories, to be propelled into the profound purposes of God.

May this be our model.

THE AROMA
OF CHRIST

For we are the aroma of Christ to God among those who are being saved
and among those who are perishing.

(2 CORINTHIANS 2:15)

I WAS IN ROW 18 on my way from Denver International to LAX in Los Angeles. The airplane was a Boeing 777, which is a large wide-body plane. It has three passenger cabins: first class, business class, and coach. Row 18 was the first row of coach.

Roughly thirty minutes into the flight, the beverage carts appeared at the front of coach class. The beverage options were presented without a snack of any kind. That meant coffee, cream, and a United Airlines napkin.

Within a few minutes I noticed that the business class section was being served as well. However, glassware was used, and food was served. Moments later the aroma of warm breakfast entrees wafted through the airplane. Although served to only a few, the fragrance enticed the entire aircraft.

I was one row away from converting the aroma into a meal. I was so close.

No one offered me their meal. No flight attendant said, "Sir, because you are so close, and because you look so hungry, I'll serve you a meal as well."

No, I paid for a coach seat and the service commensurate with coach class was all that I was going to get.

For some reason the imagery seemed especially powerful and poignant.

Our lives, lived to the full, should be an authentic reflection of what the Father has to serve. We should smell like Jesus. And in doing so, we produce a beautiful fragrance to those in our "cabin" ("those who are being saved") *and* to those who are still sitting in coach! Authentic, revealing, captivating, and attractive.

How beautiful to be able to declare to those who are drawn to the aroma that Christ has purchased a ticket in which all share that not only includes a seat in the front of the plane, but a portion of the feast as well.

A fragrance first, an invitation to the table, and a companion at the meal.

For the hungry: real food. Drawn by the fragrance, purchased by the King.

An open invitation for those in row 18 . . . and even further back.

FINISH WELL

And in the last days it shall be, God declares, that I will pour out my Spirit on all flesh, and your sons and your daughters shall prophesy, and your young men shall see visions, and your old men shall dream dreams.

(ACTS 2:17)

CLINT BOWYER IS NOT a household name for most individuals; one Sunday, however, he exploded onto television screens across the country. Bowyer is a 27-year-old from Emporia, KS who drives on the NASCAR circuit.

That Sunday at one of the most prestigious NASCAR venues, Clint Bowyer finished in eighteenth place in a field of forty-three. Unlike roughly 40 percent of the competitors, Clint finished all 202 laps. Those facts alone don't make this a more compelling story than Kevin Harvick's photo-finish victory, but in so many ways Bowyer's performance will be far more memorable for years to come. The reason is that Bowyer's number 7 Chevrolet completed the last few feet of the 500-mile race upside down and in flames. As the finish line approached, a chain reaction accident erupted just behind the front two competitors. Cars skidded, crashed, collided, and sprayed across the track and infield. But Bowyer and his Chevy pointed toward the prize. Now propelled by momentum and not traction, the car moved toward the checkered flag. Bowyer crossed the finish line, wheels in the air with sparks flying. He'd done it. All 500 miles of Daytona . . . *done.*

It's this picture—the one that is now the image on my laptop screen—that inspires me to live my Christian faith to the fullest.

One other morning I sat in the office of a man many years my senior. I witnessed a fire in Stu's soul and courage in his conviction that immediately transported me to the Bowyer image. Stu is not prepared to run life at 50 mph on cruise control, even though he'd have plenty of excuses to do just that. Instead he lives his life by the power of the Spirit and the fuel of the Great Commission. He's not in the pack—he's leading. I'm quite certain that, much like Clint Bowyer, Stu will see to it that he enters his heavenly reward with all four wheels in the air and sparks flying. It's this kind of life . . . this kind of love . . . this kind of passion that ignites something in me. Something that we were promised when the Church burst on the scene.

That's right . . . just like that. Dreaming dreams or seeing visions. I want to run this race well, from the green flag to the checkered flag. All in and all out.

Here's to finishing well . . . all 202 laps . . . all 500 miles . . . upside down and with sparks flying! Like Bowyer, but much more like my friend Stu.

WOUNDED FOR ME

He was wounded for our transgressions; he was crushed for our iniquities; upon him was the chastisement that brought us peace, and with his stripes we are healed.

(ISAIAH 53:5)

I KNOW MYSELF PRETTY well. I know that there are days that I do really stupid things. In fact, one week, I had a flight to catch for a meeting in Grand Rapids. It was a meeting that had been on the calendar for some time, with six hard-to-coordinate schedules on the other end. As I headed to the airport very early on Monday, I became increasingly aware that I had cut the time too close.

Here I was, on the morning of a big meeting with a schedule I might not be able to make. As I stood in a painfully long and slow-moving airport security line, I whispered a prayer, "Lord, please."

I had no right. It was my doing that had created the problem. The Lord hadn't set my alarm. He hadn't opted to save a few bucks and avoid the toll road. He hadn't chosen the longest security line.

As I flopped into seat 13C, a very happy passenger, I prayed a prayer of thankfulness and then a wave of overwhelming reality hit me. This answer to prayer was just a fractional example of a cosmic reality.

This episode in the Denver airport was a microcosm of God's provision in my life. The prophet Isaiah understood this so well. The Messiah, the long anticipated one, would be sent to save us by rescuing us from a mess that He hadn't created. He would get me on a flight for which I had left too late.

This reminder blitzed my mind as I sat, heart thumping, that Monday morning. Frankly, I don't like picking up the pieces when somebody else fails. I don't like paying a bill for an expense I didn't incur. I scream for justice, but plead for mercy.

He was wounded not because He sinned, not because He owed me, "not because of works done by us in righteousness, but according to his own mercy" (Titus 3:5).

What a Savior. What hope.

Jesus.

To Him be honor and glory forever.

UPHILL AND DOWN

I have learned in whatever situation I am to be content. I know how to be brought low,
and I know how to abound. In any and every circumstance, I have learned the secret
of facing plenty and hunger, abundance and need. I can do all things
through him who strengthens me.

(PHILIPPIANS 4:11-13)

I'VE LONG EMBRACED THE necessity and corresponding valor
that comes from working hard while cycling, particularly when
headed uphill. The burning in the thighs, the heaving in the lungs, the
wrestling match with my brain . . . all have inspired and propelled me.
Consequently, I've lulled myself into believing that if riding up a hill
defines me, then riding down a hill rewards me.

When the incline is in my favor, I've resolved that it is intended to
be a license to glide, to coast, to relax, maybe to breathe. And while
all of this is possible, I've begun to believe that peddling through the
downhill is important and substantial.

A lackluster downhill can cause you to lose your rhythm, to squan-
der your focus, to misplace your resolve. Coasting can lie to you. It
can make promises that a long-term journey simply will not deliver.
Coasting can make you proud of what you didn't accomplish.

This lesson forced me to confess that as with cycling, so with life. If
crisis galvanizes my resolve, then good times have a tendency to allow
that resolve to rust.

What if . . . when times are good, when things seem to be going my
way, when the hill is leaning my way, I pedaled *harder*? Would I find a
deeper sense of purpose and plan? Would I learn to know my Father

in a richer, more exhilarating way? Would I know His lavished and
extravagant grace in more compelling and humbling ways?

What if I pedaled through the downhills? What if coasting wasn't
God's idea at all?

Maybe the downhill is where the enemy does the bulk of his work.
Could it be that Satan, unable to extinguish our inferno, lulls the
coals into harmlessness by convincing us that the need for fire is over?
Complacency is certainly in his arsenal.

The apostle Paul acknowledged that he had learned "the secret" in
plenty and want. Note that he didn't say he had learned to work himself into exhaustion on the uphills and coast himself to sleep on the
downhills. He pedaled in both situations—and so should I.

I want more of Christ . . . both uphill and down.

MOVED TO AWE

Great is the LORD and greatly to be praised.

(PSALM 48:1)

THE BOOK IS CALLED *School House.* It's one of Malia's (our two-year-old granddaughter) favorites. It's one of those "Chubby Shape Books." It has eighty-five words scattered across sixteen pages, enhanced with some creative pictures.

On page seven of the book, the teacher (a glasses-wearing lamb clothed in a purple-striped dress) points to a flip chart with a picture of an elephant on it. The copy on page eight reads: *The teacher asks the children to name the animal. Can you name the animal?* (Hey, how do you get one of those writing gigs?)

For whatever reason, Malia loves this book. Every time we get to page seven, I too point to the flip chart and ask her to tell me what the animal is. Sometimes she answers; sometimes she let's me know that I need to push on to pages nine and ten.

On December 30, 2009, something incredible happened. It was on that chilly Denver night that a group of us headed to the Denver Zoo. They had more lights than animals, and more cotton candy and kettle corn than lights.

In due time we made our way to the pachyderm building. The sheer size of the crowd made us realize that something more than lights and junk food was available inside.

I scooped Malia out of the wagon that we were pulling her in and made my way through the "stink" into the building. An immediate left and we were on the railing in front of two enormous elephants. The animal on the left was drinking out of a puddle in front of it and the

monstrosity on the right was scooping up hay and shuttling it from
trunk to mouth.

Without looking at her, I admonished Malia, "Look at the elephants!" What a waste of breath! Malia was not only looking, she
was spellbound. Her mouth was literally open, jaw down, and eyes as
wide as they could possibly be. She was in awe.

We stood . . . I'm not even sure for how long. Malia's expression
never changed. No dialog, no question, no humorous explanation . . .
nothing moved her from awe.

Until December 30 at 7 p.m., Malia only thought of an elephant as
a two-dimensional, two-inch-high drawing on a flip chart page. In fact,
on page seven the elephant is smaller than the teaching lamb!

But not at the zoo. The elephant was real, and it was grand.

Is it possible that we've done our best to tame the untamable God?
Have we placed Him on page seven in a Chubby Shape Book? Is He
safe, manageable, confined?

No. He's awesome. Any and every authentic encounter with our
God will propel us to a dropped-jaw awareness.

I went to the schoolhouse myself on the thirtieth of December.
And I did it through the eyes of a two year old.

Yes, great is the Lord!

EQUIPPED TO CELEBRATE

Then Jesus was led up by the Spirit into the wilderness to be tempted by the devil.

(MATTHEW 4:1)

IN 1987, ON THE heels of winning the twenty-first Super Bowl, Phil Simms was the first to respond to the question, "Now that you've won the Super Bowl, where are you going?" His response was simply, "I'm going to Disney World." This advertising campaign has continued to echo right through Super Bowl after Super Bowl, including the same words from the mouth of Tony Dungy in 2007 as a part of the Indianapolis Colts' victory over Chicago.

It seems like a very logical question. Now that you've climbed the summit of your sport, what do you plan on doing next? How will you celebrate?

A similar question could have been asked of Jesus at the conclusion of His awesome baptism and endorsement from God. "This is my beloved Son, with whom I am well pleased" (Matthew 3:17) was the celestial announcement. You've arrived. You've been pronounced as God's own, His select, beloved.

So what's next?

With the words of God still ringing in His ears, Jesus, the only begotten, was whisked off by the Spirit into a place of isolation, solitude, discipline, and ultimately temptation. Incredible. The Disney World experience for Jesus turned out to be a showdown. Instead of a celebration, Jesus encountered the conflict of the ages.

The devil himself gave Jesus his best shot, no pulled punches, no accommodation for the fact that God had just weighed in on His identity . . . it was game on.

And I wonder . . . why do tough things happen? Why does it seem as though, at the most unexpected moments, we are ushered into the vortex?

Perhaps it's to prove that the victory itself was not a temporary lapse into a blissful condition. The endorsement of God—His declaration of our position in grace and consequently our place in His family—doesn't isolate us, but it does equip us.

Jesus, with the full radiance of the pleasure of God on His life, was led by the very Spirit of God into the wilderness to face insult, conflict, and scrutiny.

So yes, now that we've won the Super Bowl, life may be tough. We might face challenges that we never dreamed possible. But we're never, ever alone. We have a friend, a Savior, our Lord who has traveled this road before us. He knows our battle . . . He's faced it and won.

Jesus traded Disney World for a wilderness, just so He could show us the way to true and complete victory.

PACKED FOR THE TRIP

Great is our Lord, and abundant in power; his understanding is beyond measure.

(PSALM 147:5)

ONE WEEK FOR A trip to Philadelphia, I repeated a process that I have become very familiar with . . . a small roller suitcase sits on the floor of my bathroom while I look at the clothing options in my closet and decide what will fit inside the restricted space. I consider who I will be meeting with, where I will be staying, and how long I'll be gone.

Obviously, if I could fit everything I own in the suitcase, that would make the decision-making process a bit easier; I cannot. And so I decide. Sometimes well; other times, not so well.

So with a neatly packed bag I head off to Denver International Airport, never believing that I had fully packed every possible option, but confident that what I was able to fit in my suitcase will serve me well.

During the three hours that my flight took, I spent time in God's Word . . . specifically in the book of Revelation. The vastness of the descriptions, the fullness of the instruction from Jesus, the power of the words that were communicated overwhelmed me. Yet, at the same time, this incomprehensible reality provided comfort.

I realized, with renewed clarity, that the capacity of my own understanding was but a small carry-on bag in the journey. My mind, my reason, and even my heart, don't have the space to contain or fully comprehend the height, or the breath, or the richness of the God that loves me.

This reality doesn't frustrate me . . . it reassures me. Different experiences in life and different time frames will demand that my case is filled with different content. But I know that whatever the circumstance or situation, the closet is full.

I don't pretend to think that I will ever come close to containing all that God possesses, but as I study, as I pray, as I mediate on the truth of God's Word and His world, my capacity grows; my carry-on becomes a checked bag, and my awe increases.

Frustration gives way to confidence. Whatever I need is in the closet. It may not have been in my suitcase that day; after all, there were only certain things that I needed while I was in Pennsylvania. But it was there . . . for the trip to the mountains or the beach or the valley or the desert, and yes, for the trip to paradise.

Purpose in the Activity

But be doers of the word, and not hearers only, deceiving yourselves.

(James 1:22)

MY FATHER SAM WAS not a man who bagged his lawn clippings. This thought raced through my head one summer afternoon as I walked behind my own mower. I had spent significant time walking behind a mower at my boyhood home in Wheaton, Illinois where my father was the "foreman" of the job.

Sam had grown up on a farm. Function trumped aesthetics by a long shot. To that end, a lawn provided a platform for living, playing, and thriving. It was not for show or status.

Make no mistake: Sam's lawn looked nice right down to the well-trimmed bushes. But there was purpose in the activity. What we did, we did for the sake of utility. A nice yard gave us the opportunity to play catch, or to host the local whiffle ball game, or to be home base for an evening's mosquito-infested round of kick the can.

I learned at an early age that you take care of things so that they can serve you more effectively, last longer, and extend their purpose.

A well-manicured lawn can become a showpiece and not a playground. It can reject instead of invite. Sam understood that and did his best to instill it in me.

At the core this informed his theology. Results, relationships, and restoration far exceeded prestige and prominence. Sam celebrated being a "doer of the Word." He knew and respected movers and shakers, but he honored those who sacrificed. He shook the hands of dignitaries, but he washed the feet of disciples. He lauded the formidable, but he loved the missionary. He cheered for the superstar, but he wept for those on the front lines.

No, you didn't find a bag on the back of Sam's mower. It simply wasn't worth the extra investment of time when there was so much else to do.

Function before form.

No veneer, no flash, no pretense. Just purpose.

A lesson that still permeates my soul.

Stay Thirsty

O God, you are my God; earnestly I seek you; my soul thirsts for you; my flesh faints
for you, as in a dry and weary land where there is no water.

(Psalm 63:1)

WHEN SUMMER APPROACHES, SO do the dark storm clouds
that seem to descend from the Rocky Mountains by late afternoon.
Watching these clouds predictably creep out of the foothills and into
the plains of Colorado is a daily expectation. After a very dry winter
and spring, that should be a great thing. But sometimes it's not.

Even on days when you can see the dark traces of rain escaping
from the storm clouds, they often don't produce what they promise.
The phenomenon is called "virga." This is when rain falls from a cloud
but actually evaporates before it hits the ground even when the condi-
tions, the appearance, and the atmosphere seem so right.

In the book of Jude we read a stern warning about false teachers
creeping into the Church who exhibited similar behaviors. "They are
like clouds blowing over the land without giving any rain" (Jude 1:12,
NLT).

Just as the parched ground of Denver pleads with the summertime
clouds for nourishment and gets nothing, so false teachers deliver only
the appearance of good news; in reality, the refreshment evaporates
before it hits our thirsty souls. It's fluff, personally based without being biblically rooted, and so it never executes on the plans it draws up.
Yes, promising much but producing nothing.

Stay thirsty. . . .

Our souls will never know the quenching refreshment from a virga
cloud.

Thirsty? Pray for rain . . . real rain. The kind of rain with big drops: resilient, persistent, substantial drops that soak the soil of your soul. Everything else evaporates.

The God who delivers on His promises makes rain!

Joy:
The Big One

Let the rivers clap their hands; let the hills sing for joy together.

(Psalm 98:8)

WE WERE JUST MINUTES from concluding a half a day on the North Platte River in Casper, Wyoming. By all accounts it had been a good day . . . minus the successful capture of "the Big One." With the location of our disembarking in sight, I saw my strike indicator submerge with authority. A quick, but appropriate snap on my fishing pole, and I had hooked my prey.

The minutes that followed were a test of my ability to match the strength, cunning and will of this beautiful rainbow trout. This was my seventh fish of the day, and it was obviously different from the other six. The knowing gleam in the eye of Thomas, our guide, validated what I had surmised; this was a special catch.

With the fly rod bent in an unimaginable way, I hoisted the fish out of the water and toward the waiting net. With that effort, I was privy to my first and only view. And then just as quickly, my line went limp. The fish was gone . . . escaped . . . only to remain in the image snapped in my mind.

The big one. I lost the big one.

As I processed my thoughts, I was stunned by my complete lack of disappointment. Wasn't I supposed to be forlorn?

What washed over any and all sense of disappointment were some incredible images from our memorable float trip down the North Platte. It was my daughter, Alli, catching the first fish of the day with considerably more ease than was appropriate. It was Mary, my boat partner, on day one asking our guide if he would be willing to handle her beautiful catch while I took the picture. Her smile fueled me. It was the richness of the adventure, the power of the surroundings, the laughter that accompanied the expedition, the joy that intersected with each catch. I had caught the big one the moment our boats entered the water.

And so, no failed attempt could squelch what had already been deeply embraced; on the river, pole in hand, stories in the making, the big one had been landed long before.

The escape of a wonderful rainbow trout was no match for the joy I had already deposited.

Yes indeed . . . I caught the Big One.

CONSIDER THE RAVENS

Therefore I tell you, do not be anxious about your life, what you will eat, nor about your body, what you will put on. For life is more than food, and the body more than clothing. Consider the ravens: they neither sow nor reap, they have neither storehouse nor barn, and yet God feeds them. Of how much more value are you than the birds! And which of you by being anxious can add a single hour to his span of life?

(LUKE 12:22-25)

IT'S A MATTER OF odometers and jack rabbits.

I'm afraid that the statement above in many ways characterizes the core difference between my wife and me. Within two miles of our house is the Aurora Reservoir. It provides a perfect eight-mile paved loop on which we have ridden our bikes many miles.

The nicely constructed pathway creates a great environment for us to enjoy some exercise, and whatever else captures our senses.

As I confessed in the opening sentence, I am primarily focused on the statistical performance around the loop. That's why my perfectly positioned odometer provides me with just the right kind of feedback and information. Miles covered, maximum speed obtained, elapsed time, and average speed are just a few of the useful pieces of data that can be discovered with an effortless glance.

While Mary has an odometer on her bike, she rarely refers to it. Instead she consciously pans the horizon looking for any and all signs of animal life. Of particular interest to her are the fabulous jack rabbit sightings that are very infrequent, but fascinating when accomplished. Don't misunderstand; Mary is not a wildlife snob. She's delighted with a random deer, a slithering snake, or an unusual bird.

Mary doesn't miss much when we ride ... except her average speed and the miles she's covered. And me, well I miss nearly everything but my speed, distance, and average.

I've come to realize that this tendency creates a blind spot through which life drains. It is robbery at an experiential level that must be a part of what happened when we were escorted out of the garden of Eden in Genesis 3.

Frankly, it's like being ushered to a fantastic seat at an extraordinary play, only to spend the entire evening gazing at your watch. You certainly know how long each act and scene took, but you miss the power, emotion, and drama that the author intended and the actors delivered.

Consider the ravens indeed. They neither check their average speed, nor monitor their elapsed time.

I'm working toward enjoying life, one jack rabbit at a time.

READY FOR THE TEST

Therefore, my beloved, as you have always obeyed, so now, not only as in my presence but much more in my absence, work out your own salvation with fear and trembling, for it is God who works in you, both to will and to work for his good pleasure.

(PHILIPPIANS 2:12, 13)

I'M NOT SURE THAT I've ever bought a pair of used hiking boots before, but that's exactly what I did at the local REI garage sale. Consequently, I own a pair of beautiful Asolo boots.

I've certainly worn them from time to time, but never for a big one—never for a hike up a Colorado 14er (one of fifty-four 14,000-plus-foot mountains that grace this wonderful state). Last year when Mary and I did a major climb in July, I opted for my old hiking boots, because I hadn't yet broken in my Asolos.

This is precisely why I wore these boots one weekend while I spent several hours working in my basement . . . and again during the week for some work around the house. Boots, even really good boots, need to be broken in. They need to experience the unique (in my case short and wide) contour and construction of your foot.

When the apostle Paul implored the church in Philippi to "work out your own salvation," he was challenging them to "break in their boots." To test and see the fit, the contour, the strength, the grace, the power, and the personal application of their salvation. He wanted them to demonstrate faith at that time so that they would be ready for the big climbs, for the proving of their faith. As James the brother of Jesus stated: "Count it all joy, my brothers, when you meet trials of various kinds, for you know that the testing of your faith produces steadfastness" (James 1:2, 3).

So now we've set the date and we've picked the mountain: Mount Belford—14,197 feet. This time I'll wear my Asolo boots. They are tested, proven . . . and ready.

May this be true as I work out my salvation as well.

THE LOVE
OF JESUS

For the Son of Man came to seek and to save the lost.

(LUKE 19:10)

ONE WEEK I SAT on a flight to Chicago next to a four-year-old girl by the name of Zion. I describe her in the following terms: "She was disarming, bold, unafraid, and sweet." So you'll understand the complete recoil I did when I boarded the Southwest flight for my return trip from Chicago to Denver.

I was one of the last individuals on this flight. As I walked down the aisle, the flight attendant urged all of the late comers to sit in the first available middle seat. That seat proved to be 20B. The young woman in 20C seemed nice enough as I stepped past her; but in that instant I caught a detailed glimpse of the young man seated in 20A ... the window seat. Top to bottom, he was dressed in black. He wore a black-hooded sweatshirt. The hood was not only over his head, but he had pulled it down as far as he possibly could in the front. The end of the sweatshirt met jet black sunglasses that he wore for the entire flight. He had a black beard, which simply added to the monochromatic mystique of the moment. The only visible color was a patch of exposed skin on his left arm, where the sleeve of his sweatshirt had voluntarily retreated. This exposed an imposing tattoo and many, many scars from what appeared to be self-inflicted cuts.

Where was Zion, the innocent, charismatic young girl who had been my companion to Midway Airport just three days before?

My present seat partner made no sound. He never acknowledged the flight attendant; he dismissed every offer without a sound. He hunkered down in his window seat and dared anyone to enter his space. On occasion, he would reach up and tug the front of his hood further down on this face.

As I'd done three days before, I continued my journey through the Gospels. With the precision of a skillful surgeon (although without the anesthesia), the Holy Spirit did His work. Did God love this reclusive seat partner less than Zion or me? Was the love of Jesus repelled by the color black? Did the scars on an exposed left arm provide the grounds for dismissal?

Twenty minutes from Denver, he began to stir . . . and I opened the dialog: "So, is Denver your home?" It was the best I could do. To my surprise and delight, the next minutes were filled with dialog. No awkwardness, no strain—just the sense of the love of Jesus.

Enough said. . . .

HEART GUARD

Keep your heart with all vigilance, for from it flow the springs of life.

(PROVERBS 4:23)

THE DUKE PLAYER HAD no idea that a telephoto lens was catching every expression and revealing every spoken word, even though the image was disconnected from the running commentary.

This was NCAA basketball, a self-acknowledged weakness of mine. In this case, the matchup was classic, Duke and North Carolina. The situation was uncomplicated. A Duke player, a marquee talent and a mountain by human standards, was having a sub-par performance. Coach K had just subjected him to the bench, and as he went, the muted words he expressed revealed the condition of his attitude. No masterful lip reading required.

Perhaps he wouldn't have cared that a national television audience was watching what he said. The television commentators were oblivious to the rant. They were busy illuminating the obvious and enjoying their own insights. For me, the image was far more engaging and telling. The player's words propelled me to a place of reflection. When the sound is off, when I'm convinced that I'm no longer on the court, when I think no one is noticing, then, and most importantly then, what do my actions reveal? What do my "lips" expose?

From our hearts, the deep wells of our own characters, flow the reality of our personal identity. Solomon didn't challenge us to protect and guard our behavior, but our hearts.

People read our lips. They reveal our lives. They expose our character.

When the camera runs at unsuspecting times, and it does, what do people see? It's so authentic . . . it reveals so much.

King David pleaded with God, "Create in me a clean heart, O God, and renew a right spirit within me" (Psalm 51:10).

May that be our prayer and hope.

Lips that match a transformed heart . . . by His grace.

49

LIVING
THE MESSAGE

For God, who said, "Let light shine out of darkness," has shone in our hearts to give the
light of the knowledge of the glory of God in the face of Jesus Christ. But we have this
treasure in jars of clay, to show that the surpassing power belongs to God and not to us.

(2 CORINTHIANS 4: 6, 7)

WE HAD PLANNED ON a quick stop. Just a trip to the religion section of our local Borders bookstore to check on a title. When I opened the front door of the store, I was swamped with a wave of live music. A table to my right revealed the name of the group and the available CDs, but that was completely beside the point. The six members of the group were set up in the middle of the store, with full equipment, a complete sound system, and a passion to play that would have served them well in front of a crowd of thousands.

There was something about the live music. Something powerful. Something engaging. So much so that my short errand turned into a far more extended stay. Mary and I both stood just behind a rack of the latest novels, surrounded by the warmth and authenticity of real music. We clapped and participated.

Studio perfection pumping through a high-quality sound system wouldn't have stopped us, but live performers, with faces, smiles, skill, personality, and harmony interrupted our script. The subtle nuances of live music, yes, even some of the imperfection, made the sounds more captivating.

God's plan for communicating His love and truth is to use live performers. The musical score, the lyrics, and the story they tell are pure perfection. He made sure of that in His Word. And yet, He dispatches us to tell the story. Imperfect but authentic. We live lives in need of the very grace we share.

The power and purity of the message of hope is transmitted in live array through fragile, earthen containers . . . like me. But this power, this transcendent light, is lived out in person, in each of the followers of Christ. We live the message. We ache for perfection, and rightly so, but our broken lives become the instrument the Father uses to wash over the ears of a listening public.

Often God interrupts the script of those around us with authentic melody. He displays His matchless love, His abundant grace, and His transformational plan in and through me. And He does it live and in concert.

Authentic and captivating . . . jars of clay.

A CHANGE OF HEART

Therefore, confess your sins to one another and pray for one another,
that you may be healed.

(JAMES 5:16)

THE WOMAN IN 1C moved to the front of the airplane where she lingered for a few moments too long. The flight attendant insisted that she return to her seat, and as if a trigger had been pulled, the woman spouted terse, inflammatory and dismissive language at him while she returned to her seat. He returned to filling drink glasses for distribution to the passengers on flight 819. She sat in her seat, neck flushed, nonverbally reflecting her disgust.

Ten minutes later, he approached her. She was still in 1C. He leaned over so that he could address her at eye level and said, "I'm sorry about our interaction earlier." He didn't qualify the statement with a "but"; in fact, he didn't water down the statement at all. From my vantage point in seat 2D, I could see the whiplash on her face. When he had approached, she had recoiled. I'm sure that she was ready for a confrontation, for round 2 . . . and what she received instead was humility. In forty years of travel, I've never witnessed anything like it.

"I'm sorry" breathed life into a relational corpse. Humility extinguished what lightning ignited. And when that happened, just moments after it did, this brusque woman, returned the volley. "I'm sorry too," she said, with real sincerity.

It was a fragment of life, a moment, an interaction between two disconnected lives that will likely never intersect again. But for some reason, this woman received reconciliation, and an apology mattered to this flight attendant. It was moving and inspirational.

Repentance, an authentic change of heart, is powerful. It cuts across the grain of ego. It marches against the current of self-righteousness and vindication. Only to submit.

It confesses without manipulation.

It's so hard.

I stopped on my way out the door. I shook the flight attendant's hand and told him that I noticed. I told him that I thought it was noteworthy and valiant. I wanted to drink deeply of what I had witnessed at the front of a Boeing 737 bound for Denver.

Lesson learned . . . now it's my turn. Powerful words, transformational results.

TRUSTING THE INSTRUCTOR

Blessed are the poor in spirit, for theirs is the kingdom of heaven. Blessed are those who mourn, for they shall be comforted. Blessed are the meek, for they shall inherit the earth. Blessed are those who hunger and thirst for righteousness, for they shall be satisfied. Blessed are the merciful, for they shall receive mercy. Blessed are the pure in heart, for they shall see God. Blessed are the peacemakers, for they shall be called sons of God. Blessed are those who are persecuted for righteousness' sake,

(MATTHEW 5:3-10)

IT WAS MY ANNUAL golf outing . . . and it was on one of the most beautiful golf courses that I've ever played. As part of a fundraiser for the Youth for Christ military ministry, I played at the Eisenhower Course of the Air Force Academy. The scenery made up for most of the ineptitude as I worked my way through eighteen holes.

As I was leaving the registration area, a seasoned Eisenhower Course patron offered some advice. Simply put it was this, "Remember, when you are on the greens, in spite of appearances, the ball never rolls toward the mountains." While I intellectually affirmed the statement, I completely underestimated the accuracy and impact of this advice. Over and over I tested the veracity of this strategy. I amazed myself at how defiant I remained. My eyes simply wouldn't allow me to comply with the reality of the instruction. So, I putted errantly.

In Matthew 5, as Jesus begins His sermon on a mountain, He immediately launches into an instruction of contrast. A contradiction of appearances. The power of His words were tested against the backdrop of our human spirit, logic and will. In a very direct way, Jesus challenged the crowd (and us) to battle against the inclination of our minds . . . for self-reliance, for personal advancement, for notoriety, for independence, for control, for power, for safety. While these pursuits seem right, they will never bring us contentment or purpose.

Jesus knew that these words would test our will. Our minds scream at us to "putt the ball toward the mountain" when what works is just the opposite.

So, there you have it. Do you trust the Instructor? Do you believe Him when He tells you to cut across the grain, to putt away from the mountain, to defy your human tendency?

If we do, here's what Jesus promises: "Theirs is the kingdom of heaven . . . they shall be comforted . . . they shall inherit the earth . . . they shall be satisfied . . . they shall receive mercy . . . they shall see God . . . and they shall be called sons of God."

"The ball never rolls toward the mountains!"

Blessed are those of us who follow the advice of the Master for the glory of God.

THE LOST ART OF YIELDING

Not so with you. Rather, let the greatest among you become as the youngest,
and the leader as one who serves.

(LUKE 22:26)

THE RACE IS ON. In nearly every situation that I find myself, there is a rush, a press, a blitz.

Let's face it: we're an agenda-driven and a schedule-controlled people. Ask a friend how they're doing and most will respond with some variation of busy or even frantic.

We live in a world where we sprint from one congested location to the next. Traffic jams, checkout lines, security screening. Even in the privacy of our homes, our Internet connection isn't fast enough.

That's exactly why when somebody—perfect stranger or close friend—taps their brakes on our behalf, we notice . . . perhaps even marvel. We've come to believe that "yielding" is a lost art, and so we squeeze as close as we can to the car in front of us so that merging traffic has to find another option. And then there's the airport. Don't even think about it in the airport. No eye contact, that's the first part of the strategy. Step up. Step in. It's all about bin space, making con-nections, retrieving luggage . . . it's all about me . . . first.

Jesus treasured brake tappers. He tried to get His disciples to understand that when somebody was prepared to interrupt their own agenda or traffic pattern for the sake of someone else . . . then they were getting closer to understanding the heart of sacrifice that He was all about.

"You first." "Go ahead." "After you." "I'll wait." "You take it."

The transformation of the heart changes our place in line. Followers of Jesus . . . well . . . they follow. They embrace the "last will be first, and the leader as one who serves" way of life (Luke 22:24-27).

Imagine what would happen if the people of God became known as the brake tappers. Project what the world would think if we were the ones who made room for others. Just think what it would mean if we intentionally made eye contact so that we could deliver mercy and grace.

Jesus had a description for this kind of selfless, sacrificial, generous living . . . He said it was "a beautiful thing" (Mark 14:6).

It pleases Him when we set our agenda aside. He delights when we yield. He celebrates when we have the courage to say no to ourselves . . . even in a grocery store line.

Even Jesus, especially Jesus, made room for line cutting, me first, don't-cut-me-off kind of people like me. Wouldn't He love it if I did the same?

. . . After you.

"DEESE"

As he was getting into the boat, the man who had been possessed with demons begged him that he might be with him.

(MARK 5:18)

"DEESE." THIS WORD IS typically the companion to a pointed finger as my two-year-old granddaughter attempts to communicate that she wants something. I think she's saying "this." The intensity of her request is often combined with a quick swipe of her right hand across her chest as she signs the word "please."

When Malia wants something, you know.

Her unmasked passion for "more" and her need for help propel her toward the exposed expression of her heart. By contrast, my muted desires and self-sufficiency hide . . . and most likely dull . . . the craving for more. Self-control has given way to lowered expectations and I confine what needs to be liberated.

Consequently, the "fire in my belly" becomes a controlled burn. I constrain what should be unleashed. I'm afraid to ask for "deese," for "more," because I might be disappointed, or I might not understand God's plan . . . so I stop short. I harness. I confine my requests to what I can conceive of as attainable. And as a result, I miss something . . . perhaps I miss everything.

I miss the explosion of God's miraculous power. I miss the "peace of God which surpasses all understanding" (Philippians 4:7), because I've put borders around the disappointment.

More. Please more.

Of Jesus. Of His Kingdom. Of His people. Of His call. Of His heart. Of intimacy with Him.

A soul set free wants more. An unleashed heart begs to be with Jesus. For "deese."

What if I were prepared to embrace the uncertainty that comes from asking? What if I trusted my Father to sift through the providence of the request . . . but never to disqualify the passion because of feasibility? What if I took all of the "deese" to the Father and I let Him be God? What if . . . I stoked the embers of my fire . . . and I admitted that I need help? What if?

More . . . so much more.

Please.

A TIMELY
REMINDER

I came that they may have life and have it abundantly.

(John 10:10)

I'VE BEEN TO RENTAL car counters a great deal over the last four and a half years . . . in fact, three times in one week. But recently, at Midway Airport in Chicago, something unexpected provided a measure of inspiration and perspective that was significant.

It was at the precise moment where my patience was at its breaking point that the man behind the counter looked at me and said, "Sir, do you still live on Davies Way?" I nodded as politely as I could and said yes. And then he said, "And sir, do you still work for Youth for Christ?" And again, I responded with a yes. But what followed was off the script. It was as though my affirmative answer had pushed the needle out of the groove and, in an instant, the rental car agent was freelancing. "Wow," he said. "What an important job you have."

Oblivious to my personal title, and unaware of any specific responsibility, our organizational brand captivated the heart of a man who lives in a city where youth violence and hatred seem to be racing out of control. I felt as though I had just delivered a vaccine to a disease-infested region. I had the answer to a troubling problem ... to *the* troubling problem.

As quickly as the agent had been thrust off course, he delivered the same propulsion for me. It took seconds to derail me from the rhythm of another routine airport experience and into the powerful reality of God's amazing plan.

"Our kids need this!" he added as he continued to reflect on the power of a name and the significance of the promise it delivers.

With paperwork in hand, I thanked the gentleman behind the counter. But thanks didn't seem enough. In a momentary encounter, through a spontaneous response, in the middle of a scripted routine, the significance of God's plan broke through and reminded me of the powerful truth that Christ, and Christ alone, can lay siege to the fortress of hatred, violence, and hopelessness that permeates the culture. He alone offers abundant life.

At a rental car counter. Not while I poured over Scripture, not while I listened to a powerful and tightly orchestrated sermon. At the rental counter, God broke through.

When we bring the hope of Jesus to a broken world, we are doing what's important, what Jesus commanded and modeled. And when we grasp that, even in an instant ... everything looks different.

CREATE A ROAR

Beware of practicing your righteousness before other people in order to be seen by them,
for then you will have no reward from your Father who is in heaven.

(MATTHEW 6:1)

BUCKLEY AIR FORCE BASE is twelve miles from our house. This means that frequently we are on the flight pattern for fighter jets taking off. The roar is unmistakable: powerful and fierce.

While the noise created from the powerful jet engines is captivating, the visual image of the airplane is illusive. The reason for this is simple. When I am interrupted by the sound of a fighter, I immediately look to the location where I am hearing the sound. The problem is that the incredible speed of the airplane propels it well ahead of the sound. If I'm chasing the airplane by following the sound, I'll never catch up.

The flight path of the jet precedes the auditory impact that it leaves. The airplane is "gone" by the time we recognize its presence.

I'm convinced that this description matches well the life lived by Jesus . . . and it instructs our lives as well.

The powerful force of Jesus' earthly existence—the sonic boom of His love, His teaching, and His behavior—roared through history long after His image was gone, long after His body ascended into the eternal presence of His Father.

Godly, honorable, humble leaders are most distinctly known by the intensity of the roar that trails behind a life well lived.

If you look at the profound impact that significant leaders have had throughout history, the sound will most often be far from the individuals themselves. The transformation trails behind. Real change lingers behind the catalyst that creates it.

A leader who expects the noise to surround his or her life is not really interested in progress. He or she is interested in fame and recognition. A servant leader understands and expects that it will be long after he or she is gone that people will most appreciate the full impact and force of his or her life.

It's not until Jesus announces, "Well done, good and faithful servant" (Matthew 25:21) that the sound will catch up to the image—when the lag time is gone, when the invisible is brought to light.

Find joy in living a life that creates a roar miles and miles behind you.

THE SMELL
OF HEAVEN

*The twenty-four elders fell down before the Lamb, each holding a harp, and golden
bowls full of incense, which are the prayers of the saints.*

(REVELATION 5:8)

I WAS JUST A few hours from walking back into my house after
being on the road for several days. When that happens, when I walk
from the garage into the laundry room, I am usually greeted with a
smell. It's the smell of our home. It's familiar and comforting. An ag-
gregation of things makes the smell, but it's the way our house smelled
in Kansas City, in Goshen, in Nashville, and in Fort Wayne. I love the
smell . . . and when I'm away, I miss it.

I believe that longing for the smell of home is not only okay, it's biblical. In fact, the book of Revelation reveals that the smells of heaven
will be produced, in part, from the incense of God's people. Scripture
records that the golden bowls of the elders will be full of incense. And
then it gives us the formula for the incense. The secret ingredients.

The smell of heaven, the aroma before the Almighty, the fragrance
that creates the comfort of home eternal, is the ignited prayers of the
saints. These are authentic prayers. A "rock concert of praise" prayers.
Gut-wrenching, desperate prayers. Tear-stained, painful prayers.
Laughter-infused, celebration prayers. Worn-out, consistent prayers.
Frustration-laced, honest prayers. Blood-stained, in-the-middle-of-
the-battle, warrior prayers. Hope-filled, peace-saturated, wilderness
prayers. And they, without artificial perfume, are the wonderful smells
of home. They are smells that will remind us of those who have
prayed much.

So pray. Pray with passion and power, knowing that as you do, you infiltrate the atmosphere of heaven, that you impact eternity. Be confident that these prayers become a gift before the throne, a fitting offering to the Lamb.

Is it any wonder why I love the smell of home?

Pray.

FAITHFUL UP-HILL AND DOWN

His master said to him, "Well done, good and faithful servant. You have been faithful over a little; I will set you over much. Enter into the joy of your master."

(MATTHEW 25:21)

I'VE LONG BEEN DRAWN to the speedometer that is attached to the handlebar of my bicycle. I confess . . . to a fault.

My multi-function Cateye brand gage is a powerful little tool. It provides useful feedback both during and after a ride. Perhaps the most significant function provided by this handy device is the cadence monitor. A sensor is connected to my pedal and the display on my handlebar shows me just how many rotations of the pedals occur in a one-minute period. In cycling communities, this is *the* number to watch.

To ride at the proper rpms is a huge factor in fatigue, in physical wear and tear, in prolonged cycling performance, and in an ability to face the varied challenges that any ride will produce.

According to most journals and experts, the optimal rotations per minute are 80 to 85. Yes . . . that's right . . . 80 to 85. For most individuals this is really spinning. Lance Armstrong, the most famous current cyclist in the world, prefers to ride at 90 to 95 rpms.

With modern bikes and the improved gear technology, it's possible to ride at 80 rpms both uphill and down. This means that optimally, your legs are pumping at relatively the same rate in all circumstances.

Just yesterday on a little ride in the country, I worked to stay right at 80 rpms. On a beautiful Colorado downhill, I was pumping away at my optimal rate at a speed of 36 mph. Moments later I was repaying the "downhill loan" and I was still pumping at 80 rpms, but I was only traveling at 9.9 mph.

Cadence is more important than speed.

We all can remember the days when we strained with every ounce of energy that we had to pedal up a neighborhood hill. We falsely believed that the veins popping out of our neck and other signs of strain showed that we were diligent, committed, tough and successful. Wrong!

Life, like cycling, throws a wide variety of terrains our way. Few days, let alone weeks or years, are flat and predictable. Often, and wrongly so, we assume that followers of Jesus should always travel at the same speed. We keel over in exhaustion, we quit in frustration, we disbelieve that we can learn from difficult situations, and we coast when we should still be pedaling.

Our Father is more concerned with cadence than speed. Pain, disappointment, suffering, and doubt can't be traversed at the same velocity as celebration and success.

In biblical terms, I believe that cadence equates to faithfulness. Faithful uphill and down. Faithful in plenty and want. Eighty rpms.

Our Father gives us many beautiful and practical ways to shift gears. His Word, His Church, His Spirit—all work to constrain, release, or encourage us at the proper time in our journey.

Well done for faithfulness, not for velocity. For commitment uphill and down. Steady. Strong. Cadence . . . not our speed. Keep at 80 rpms: faithful.

SELAH

God is our refuge and strength, a very present help in trouble. Therefore we will not fear though the earth gives way, though the mountains be moved into the heart of the sea, though its waters roar and foam, though the mountains tremble at its swelling. Selah.

(PSALM 46:1-3)

SELAH. THIS HEBREW WORD appears seventy times in the book of Psalms, and although there is some debate about the precise meaning, it's universally agreed that the term applies to the musical construct of this poetic masterpiece. It's believed that it invites an interlude or pause in the midst of the honest dialog.

For instance:

You are a hiding place for me; you preserve me from trouble; you surround me with shouts of deliverance. Selah.

(PSALM 32:7)

God is our refuge and strength, a very present help in trouble. Therefore we will not fear though the earth gives way, though the mountains be moved into the heart of the sea, though its waters roar and foam, though the mountains tremble at its swelling. Selah

(PSALM 46:1)

Each psalmist knew that a pause was the next important element in the journey with the Father.

Wikipedia (the free online encyclopedia) has this to say about the word: "*Selah* may be the most difficult word in the Hebrew Bible to translate. It is probably either a liturgico-musical mark or an instruction on the reading of the text, something like 'stop and listen.'"

Stop and listen. That captures the beauty and the power of this five-letter word. *Selah*. In a cruise control, microwave, wireless, cellular, iPod, Internet, information-smothering world, a pause. *Selah*.

And so, on a Sunday morning, Mary and I filled our van with bikes, books, and boots and headed into the mountains for a week. Yes, a week . . . of *selah*. A time to stop and to listen.

Our Lord knows . . . noise doesn't do what rest alone can. So pause. Rest. Wait and listen. Turn it off. Unplug it. Leave it uncharged. *Selah*.

GOD WAS RIGHT

The LORD God took the man and put him in the garden of Eden to work it and keep it. And the LORD God commanded the man, saying, "You may surely eat of every tree of the garden, but of the tree of the knowledge of good and evil you shall not eat, for in the day that you eat of it you shall surely die."

(GENESIS 2:15-17)

THE DEATHS OF HIGH-PROFILE individuals dominated the pages of our newspapers, the radio airwaves, and the television broadcasts over a couple of weeks. The end of a human life captures us in a way that few other events do.

I think I understand why. It is on the battleground of life and death that we inescapably encounter God. It was on this landscape that God's credibility, and indeed, His character were challenged. As we inspect this confrontation we see that even here God is validated. And ultimately, death provides the stage on which His magnificent love and hope are exposed.

Now the serpent was more crafty than any other beast of the field that the LORD God had made. He said to the woman, "Did God actually say, 'You shall not eat of any tree in the garden'?" And the woman said to the serpent, "We may eat of the fruit of the trees in the garden, but God said, 'You shall not eat of the fruit of the tree that is in the midst of the garden, neither shall you touch it, lest you die.'" But the serpent said to the woman, "You will not surely die."

(GENESIS 3:1-4)

The showdown: "You shall die," vs. "You will not surely die."

The gauntlet has been dropped, the ground rules have been established, the criteria for evaluation has been clearly set.

Both God and Satan cannot be right; the middle ground has long since been traversed: "Thus all the days that Adam lived were 930 years, and he died" (Genesis 5:5).

Adam died.

Certainly it didn't take 930 years for Adam to know that he was wrong. In fact, that happened in an instant . . . his soul told him in unmistakable ways. But history declares with indisputable clarity that God was right. With sin and defiance came death. And with death came a clear declaration that God was, and is, right.

In a painful, gut-wrenching way, when we hear about death, our souls proclaim that God was right, that His perfect character was never in question. That He is not to be trifled with or dismissed. That ultimately, the gift of His perfect Son was His way of ushering us back to the garden, to a place of relationship with Him, to beauty and peace that will never be experienced without the Lamb.

Even death screams for God.

No to the
Whisper

Peter took him aside and began to rebuke him, saying, "Far be it from you, Lord! This shall never happen to you." But he turned and said to Peter, "Get behind me, Satan! You are a hindrance to me. For you are not setting your mind on the things of God, but on the things of man."

(MATTHEW 16:22, 23)

THIS PAST YEAR, I have worked to make push-ups a regular part of my daily routine. I've done so with varying degrees of regularity, but have steadily been able to sense the impact on my physical condition. But this past Monday, something happened. I was mid-workout and clicking through my regiment with about thirty push-ups to go. At a moment of downward plunge, my mind started to betray me. Although I had done the repetitions before, the messages from my brain started to go something like this:

"Wow, this feels like more work than normal. I wonder what's different today. Yikes, I'm not sure I can get all the way to my goal. In fact, I'm pretty sure that's just not possible today."

And in that instant, my mind gave my body permission to quit. I had done the full rationalization; I had my excuse ready and my compromise in hand. I had done enough. And so, that's what I did. I stopped. Sure, my heart was pounding and I was appropriately winded, but I wasn't done.

I had given in to the traitor.

Jesus understood this tendency. In fact, He confronted it and defeated it. In doing so, He showed us the way. On one occasion the quitter's voice He heard came from Peter. Just after Peter's wonderful confession of Jesus as the Messiah, he rebukes Jesus for suggesting that He would die.

When your mind starts to whisper words that give you permission to quit, echo back the stunning words of Jesus: "Get behind me, Satan! You are a hindrance to me. For you are not setting your mind on the things of God, but on the things of man."

Never be content to stop short of God's ideal for you, not even one push-up short. Rely on the Holy Spirit to motivate and equip you for the challenges you face.

In the words of Winston Churchill in 1941: "Never give in. Never give in. Never, never, never, never—in nothing, great or small, large or petty—never give in, except to convictions of honor and good sense. Never yield to force. Never yield to the apparently overwhelming might of the enemy."

May we be honest enough to confess our weakness, strong enough to ask for help, and courageous enough to cling to the hope that propels us . . . through one more push-up, past one more temptation, through fear, past despair, all the way to a bloodstained cross and an empty tomb.

Even Jesus had to say "no" to the whisper. . . .

Honestly, hopefully, courageously.

BATTLING TOGETHER

There was a man of great stature, who had six fingers on each hand, and six toes on each foot, twenty-four in number. . . . And when he taunted Israel, Jonathan the son of Shimei, David's brother, struck him down.

(2 SAMUEL 21:20, 21)

DID YOU KNOW THAT **King David** had the opportunity to square off with giants on multiple occasions? While the sling-wielding encounter with the trash-talking enemy described in 1 Samuel 17 gets the bulk of the sermon headings, there were others that confronted the king throughout his life. In particular, the second book of Samuel, the twenty-first chapter, describes a nameless giant.

This giant taunted the people of God as well. But it's his physical description that has riveted me. A giant, outrageous in size, and un-relenting in grasp. Six fingers on each hand will do that for you. This is an enemy that won't simply let go with a casual flick of the wrist. I picture a man the human equivalent of a vise-grip tool. And when I picture the challenge of 2 Samuel 21, I picture the powerful, persis-tent, and painful enemy that confronts me. In a word . . . worry.

In fact, there are days when I'm convinced that this giant actually grows additional fingers overnight. There are phone calls, conversa-tions, or reports that seem to define in clearer terms just how daunt-ing the situation is.

Much like David, this takes me to a place where I need help. Un-like the battle with Goliath, David didn't single-handedly defeat this giant. Actually his nephew, the son of his brother, stepped into the fray. His name was Jonathan, and although we don't know a great deal about him, we know that he "struck him down" (2 Samuel 2:21). He intervened. He confronted the vise-grip on behalf of his uncle ... on behalf of his God.

Like David, my plea for help is not ignored. The worry that at times squeezes so tightly is confronted head on by others who stand beside me. By others who have more faith, others who have less fear, others who know the power of our God much better.

I can't fight this giant alone. God never intended for me to do so. Family and friends become warriors and comrades. Their courage is applied to my battle, and God works in them, with them, through them ... to liberate and love.

There is no enemy, no grip that confounds our God or overwhelms His people. Together. We can release the captive for the sake of the King.

ENOUGH

It is enough; now, O LORD, take away my life, for I am no better than my fathers.

(1 KINGS 19:4)

EVEN ELIJAH . . .

The courageous servant of God. The man whom God had fed and cared for in the desert. The man whom God used to raise the son of a widow from the dead. The prophet who went toe to toe with 450 prophets of Baal and 400 prophets of Asherah. The man who called down the consuming power of God to lap up the water and the doubts of the enemies of God. As an old man, he had outrun the horses of Ahab in a seventeen-mile race to Jezreel. He had witnessed and participated in the overt work of God. Yet even Elijah got to a place in his life where he cried out to the Almighty, even while he stood in the center of God's will.

"It's enough," he lamented.

He had seen the hand of God in subtle and gentle ways, and in blatant and extravagant circumstances, but he, the hand-picked prophet, got to the end of his rope.

Even Elijah . . .

It's easy to imagine that when we are squarely in the center of God's will, we will never doubt, never get discouraged, and never want to give up.

That might be true if a walk with God provided the entrance ramp to easy street; but it doesn't. In fact, it may produce exactly the opposite. John 15 records the words of Jesus predicting hatred from the world for His followers. In John 16 Jesus once again announces the fact that we will have tribulation.

And with the overt and covert attacks, we will be tempted to sit under a broom tree (1 Kings 19:5) and give up. "*Enough!* I've had all that I can take!"

We will want to retreat to a cave and be tempted to stay there; yet even there, the pursuing love of a faithful God extends to us. "What are you doing here, Elijah?" (1 Kings 19:9)

Even Elijah . . .

Are you feeling discouraged? You don't doubt your call . . . just your resolve. You wonder if you can go one more week, or one more day, or one more hour. God seems silent, removed, distant.

Even Elijah . . .

Tell God. Tell Him what you're feeling. Tell Him what it's like to be you.

And behold, the LORD passed by, and a great and strong wind tore the mountains and
broke in pieces the rocks before the LORD, but the LORD was not in the wind.
And after the wind an earthquake, but the LORD was not in the earthquake.
And after the earthquake a fire, but the LORD was not in the fire.
And after the fire the sound of a low whisper.

(1 KINGS 19:11-13)

Then . . . listen for the whisper.

LIVE
GENEROUSLY

Each one must give as he has decided in his heart,
not reluctantly or under compulsion,
for God loves a cheerful giver.

(2 CORINTHIANS 9:7)

MARY AND I WERE just outside of Cheyenne, Wyoming on our way to Casper when she spotted a sign for a Starbucks. "Let's stop. I'll buy!"

The offer from Mary was spontaneous, genuine . . . and then humorous. The Starbucks card that Mary planned on using when we made the stop was a card that I had given her a couple of years ago. It's one of the cards that allows you to periodically add funds to your "coffee balance." I had done just that three weeks before our trip. Without being ungrateful, I looked at Mary and reminded her of the fact that the "buying" that she was going to do was a product of the "investing" that I had done. There was something about the moment that made us both laugh.

But this reality sat in my mind like a broken-down car on the side of the road.

Mary had offered back to me the opportunity to participate in something that I had entrusted to her. She had full sway over the direction of these assets. They were hers to dispense. So when she gave them back, they had *more* meaning, not less.

In that moment I experienced a miniscule sense of what God, our Father, feels when we open-handedly give back to Him what He so generously lavished on us. When we serve, give, love, show compassion, weep with those who weep, and rejoice at the goodness of our God, we are buying a cup of coffee with the funds the Father has put into our account. And remarkably, it brings God joy.

You buy. And when you do, there is delight for our Father.

My card; His resources. Live generously.

Teach Us to Number Our Days

The years of our life are seventy, or even by reason of strength eighty; yet their span is but toil and trouble; they are soon gone, and we fly away. Who considers the power of your anger, and your wrath according to the fear of you? So teach us to number our days that we may get a heart of wisdom.

(Psalm 90:10-12)

I WAS LATE FOR my flight, and worried that I might have to sort through plan B for making it from Portland to Detroit. Complicating matters was the fact that I had a rental car to return.

As I approached the unfamiliar airport, I quickly scanned for signs that would point me toward the return of my rental car. It was a quick left-hand exit and then a ramp to the second floor of the airport garage. My heart raced as my mind charted a path through the check-in process. The variables ahead of me made the certainty of my outcome questionable. Kiosks working? Security lines? Crowds? And so much more.

I quickly caught the *Return Lane* sign for Budget Rental and whipped my car into a space behind the last car in line. To add to my growing optimism, I saw a man with a handheld device approaching the car.

By this point I was out of the vehicle and on my way to retrieve my cases from the trunk.

"Sir," the attendant's voice broke my concentration. "Sir, this isn't our car."

In the few seconds that followed I was informed—actually reminded—that the car that I was returning had been rented from Dollar and not from Budget.

This was a self-inflicted wound. I had nobody to blame, no phone number to call, no company to write, no clerk to persuade . . . this was on me, and me alone.

The minutes were precious and I had just exchanged them carelessly. In fact, I threw away ten of them before I got everything back to its rightful place. . . .

Wasn't I the one who wrote about the "courage to go slow"? Weren't those my fingers that typed those words?

So I write from detention. Yes, I have much to learn about moving at the "pace of wisdom."

So again . . . I confess . . . life, most typically, is a rush. From one activity, from one airport, from one appointment, from one assignment, from one crisis, from one conversation . . . to the next.

And somewhere in all of this, while I'm still in the fast lane, I drive right past thoughtfulness and wisdom . . . only to need it desperately a few minutes later.

I'm learning. Slowly . . . but I'm learning.

Take time . . . take time today to move slowly enough to put things back in the right place.

From the remedial side of the classroom, I join you in this journey.

WORDS WITHOUT KNOWLEDGE

Who is this that darkens counsel by words without knowledge?

(Job 38:2)

ONE THOUSAND, EIGHT HUNDRED and sixty-one words. . . .

Eloquent, at times poetic, powerful . . . and completely empty.

Eliphaz the Temanite was one of the "friends" of Job. The lead friend.

In his rush to judge, in his desire to unravel, in his passion to fit Job's circumstances inside the context of his own theology, he spewed 1,861 words of condemnation, shame, rejection, and misunderstanding.

"My anger burns against you . . . for you have not spoken of me what is right" (Job 42:7). This from the mouth of God!

Eliphaz raced to put a bow on the scrap heap of Job's circumstances. In doing so, he exposed his own ignorance. He also failed his friend.

Vulnerable and tender, Job was an easy target for Eliphaz and his assassin bullets. Eliphaz's inability to comprehend the mind of God hijacked his good intentions and subjugated them to the need to defend God, to explain the unexplainable. His actions took him to a place that shone the light on similar tendencies in my own heart and mind.

Blame dispensed and judgment delivered . . . and the pain, the vacuum, and the grief swelled. Eliphaz misunderstood the shoulders of God. He narrowed them, shrinking them to a width that fit neatly inside of his need to protect the reputation of the Almighty.

God needed no such deliverance. His shoulders are broad. His mercy is new. His love is infinite. His hope is boundless. No bows are necessary . . . just honesty, vulnerability, and authenticity.

Recently I fear that I have been Eliphaz to family, to friends. With my lips and in my heart . . . I've acted as a bodyguard for the Almighty. How absurd.

Words without knowledge. . . .

"Father, forgive me for the times that I have reached for the script of Eliphaz instead of the arms of Jesus. Your ego is not fragile; your shoulders are not narrow. Forgive me."

Needing His grace, extending His love, awed by His power.

PACK LIGHT

He called the twelve and began to send them out two by two, and gave them authority
over the unclean spirits. He charged them to take nothing for their journey except a
staff—no bread, no bag, no money in their belts—but to wear sandals
and not put on two tunics.

(MARK 6:7-9)

DOWN IN MY BASEMENT I have a corner where I store my hiking gear. It simplifies the process of making certain that I will have all that I need when Mary and I embark on an outdoor adventure. Backpack, water bottles, first aid kit, compass, trail maps, a knee brace, our Colorado 14er book (which gives valuable insight into all fifty-four mountains in Colorado that have an elevation of over 14,000 feet), an oxygen bottle, and yes, a can of bear repellent (never used, but always available . . . peace of mind in an aerosol can!). Preparation is vital.

That's why I find the words of Jesus in Mark 6:7-9 to be so stunning.

Let's understand this: the disciples, dispatched for duty, aware of the uncertainty of the assignment, constrained to move by the Spirit. And the packing checklist looked like this:

No food.

No luggage.

No money.

No extra clothing.

The disciples had to be stunned. "Take nothing." But make no mistake; Jesus had a perfect strategy and an ideal design. This was not a suicide mission or a haphazard approach. Jesus fully equipped the disciples.

Each disciple, mission clearly spelled out, was released with two incredible resources: authority and companionship. These were the key components to successfully executing the call of God. Perhaps this very lesson was still ringing in the ears of Peter when he wrote, "His divine power has granted to us all things that pertain to life and godliness, through the knowledge of him who called us to his own glory and excellence" (2 Peter 1:3).

We have all things necessary for the journey and the call when we embrace His divine power, when we dip deeply into the well of His authority and rely humbly on the companions that share our pathway. Notice that Peter selected the word "us" when he described the call. This is not a solo mission, and it's not fueled by fumes.

Together and with power.

This is the formula: Pack light, but pack wisely.

REJECT THE WHISPER

A river flowed from the land of Eden, watering the garden and then dividing into four branches. The first branch, called the Pishon, flowed around the entire land of Havilah, where gold is found. The gold of that land is exceptionally pure; aromatic resin and onyx stone are also found there.

(GENESIS 2:10-12, NLT)

EDEN WAS GLORIOUS. RIVERS, vegetation that flourished, fruit that exploded with taste and beauty. Gems, fragrance, companionship and interpersonal dialog with the Almighty. Yet, in the midst of the perfection and beauty . . . boundaries.

God placed a perimeter around a tree in the center. It would have been much easier if this tree had been despicable. But I sense that this was a fabulous tree with radiant and attractive fruit. Even the name of the tree was powerful and magnetic: "the tree of the knowledge of good and evil." It might have been better if God had named it something like "the death-delivering, life-sucking, relationship-destroying, God-separating weed." But no, this was not His plan.

Everything about this tree was attractive, and to make matters worse, it was unavoidable . . . it was in the middle of the garden.

I would guess that even the fruit tasted good. There was no allergic reaction, no instant vomiting, no repulsive sensation . . . just the poison of the soul, sin. This is exactly why sin is sin. It's often not hideous; in fact, it may be downright beautiful and accessible. But it's also wrong. It's on the other side of the boundary.

The garden has so much that's right, so much that's glorious and life giving. But there is still the tree, the one beautiful tree in the middle.

And with the tree, a whisper, the tantalizing promise, the lie: "You will not really die."

The fruit on the tree led to separation, pain, disappointment, stupid little fig-leaf excuses for an existence . . . and to death.

The garden or the tree? Inside the boundaries or out? God's masterpiece was turned loose to reject Him or to bring Him glory and to enjoy Him forever. When we start defending the tree instead of enjoying the garden, then we'll know that we're really naked.

Reject the whisper. . . . Enjoy the garden.

87

CONVICTION: A PAINFUL EXERCISE

When Simon Peter saw it, he fell down at Jesus' knees, saying, "Depart from me, for I am a sinful man, O Lord."

(LUKE 5:8)

A RESPITE FROM THE winter days of Denver, and Mary and I were on our bikes for a Saturday ride. It was wonderful to pedal around the Aurora Reservoir side by side.

The culmination of our ride is a final quarter-mile incline that takes us to a stoplight close to our house. It might be that I'm overly competitive, but I like to push hard over the final stretch. On that Saturday, I did just that. Because exercise had been little and far between, my body screamed at me. My thighs burned and my lungs heaved as I pumped as hard as I could. At the halfway point into the sprint, my mind had to declare its resolve to my body. I wanted to quit, to back down, to establish a rationale for a shortened victory. But I pushed through. I invited the discomfort. I welcomed the misery.

Later, in the quietness of my morning time in the Word, I felt a twinge of conviction as I read the masterful and powerful words of Jesus in Luke 5:1-11. His invitation to the first disciples pierced my own heart. I was getting uncomfortable. The muscles of my heart and soul were being extended. My body screamed for a shortcut, an early exit. "Move on quickly!" But with the resolve that only the Holy Spirit can bring, I pressed on. I welcomed the discomfort, I embraced the sting. "Convict me. . . . Make me more like You. . . . Push into the deepest parts of my soul with Your power and light."

Up the hill. Through the desperate gasps. Past the halfway point.

Conviction is the deep and painful exercise of the soul. It extends and increases our capacity to know and love God. It tests our resolve and displaces our self-deception. It's uncomfortable, but vital to our spiritual health.

Climb. Dig deep. Declare to your body that you won't quit halfway through.

BE STRONG AND COURAGEOUS

*Be strong and courageous. Do not be frightened, and do not be dismayed, for the Lord
your God is with you wherever you go.*

(Joshua 1:9)

Moses my servant is dead.

(Joshua 1:2)

That's right Joshua. The baton is now firmly in your hand. The
Promised Land is in front of you and the emergency brake that I
locked in place for Moses has been released. The expansive resources
of this land are now available to you, to My people.

*Every place that the sole of your foot will tread upon I have given to you,
just as I promised to Moses.*

(Joshua 1:3)

That's right Joshua. You're the guy. You're My guy. I want you to
step out. To march forward into the uncertainty with the confidence
that "every place" is yours. It's yours because it's Mine. The fire that
I ignited in your soul when you first scouted the land can now be
fanned into a blaze. Move. Occupy. No dream is too big. No territory
too untamed. Every place means every place.

*No man shall be able to stand before you all the days of your life. Just as I was with
Moses, so I will be with you. I will not leave you or forsake you.*

(Joshua 1:5)

That's right Joshua. No man. Not a giant. Not a political leader, not a military power, not a shrewd strategist . . . no man. And not just for tomorrow or the next day . . . but for all of the days of your life. I'm here. Permanently.

This Book of the Law shall not depart from your mouth, but you shall meditate on it day and night, so that you may be careful to do according to all that is written in it. For then you will make your way prosperous, and then you will have good success.

(Joshua 1:8)

That's right Joshua. Camp on My Word. Set your mind, your heart, and your soul on the things that I've communicated to you through My Word. Use it, not as a reference book, but as a guide for life.

Be strong and courageous. Do not be frightened, and do not be dismayed, for the Lord your God is with you wherever you go.

(Joshua 1:9)

That's right Joshua. Strong. Courageous. Confident. Liberated. Wherever you go.

I can almost hear God saying, "That's right, Dan. That baton is yours. It's time to occupy the promises of God. It's time to cross the river of doubt, of uncertainty . . . and take possession of what I have already given to you."

The Lord our God is strong and mighty. He has not lost His power to do more than I could ask or imagine.

God is stirring. Now, as then. God ignites the dream.

Be strong and courageous.

BE A BONFIRE

This is why I remind you to keep using the gift God gave you when I laid my hands on you. Now let it grow, as a small flame grows into a fire. God did not give us a spirit that makes us afraid but a spirit of power and love and self-control.

(2 TIMOTHY 1:6, 7, NCV)

HAVE YOU EVER WALKED past an open fire that wasn't yours? I mean you didn't build it, you aren't tending it, you weren't involved in providing the necessary fuel to ignite or sustain it. But you walked by it, and when you did, you instantly felt the heat that it produced. You may or may not have acknowledged it, and you may or may not have paused and wandered closer; regardless, you felt the heat.

For those of us who claim the name of Christ and desire to follow Him faithfully, this image should be inspirational. In fact, it is the way that Jesus lived His life on earth. His actions, His interactions, and His insights provided warmth not only to those who were huddled around the fire of His life, but to passersby as well. In fact, it was often those on the periphery who were attracted the most magnetically to the heartbeat of Jesus. They felt the heat before they embraced the fire.

I've begun to systematically confront the notion in my mind that my job as a Christian in our society is to somehow scorch the evil right out of our culture. I used to think of myself as a flamethrower. Now I have a different picture, one that's not only more inviting to others, but frankly, one that generates significantly more heat than the old model.

I want my life to be a bonfire of grace and love. I want the flames to generate warmth, not only for friends and family, but for strangers and skeptics. I want my life to warm hearts as a part of the process of the Spirit igniting them.

I want the brokenness, disappointment, challenges, and joys of my life to provide ample kindling for the kind of fire that attracts and engages.

Using the gifts that God has given me, I want to be a beautiful bonfire of grace, humility, and love. I believe that warmth captivates rigid, lifeless, and cold hearts, perhaps most often of those who just happen to cross my path, who just happen to wander past the fire.

Warmth, then fire.

COMPLETE
IN HIM

For in Christ lives all the fullness of God in a human body.
So you also are complete through your union with Christ.

(COLOSSIANS 2:9, 10, NLT)

IT WAS A GREAT Christmas party. Our national staff and several local staff members who were in Denver for training and vision casting joined together for a time of celebration.

After everyone had left, Mary and I were cleaning up a few final dishes in the kitchen and I offered to clean the two coffee pots that I had been responsible to fill a few hours before.

When I pulled the first pot to the sink, I was surprised by the weight of the urn. It felt amazingly heavy. When I removed the cover of the sixty-cup percolator, I answered the question that the unexpected weight had created. Everything—the ground coffee, the clean clear water in the bottom—were exactly as they had been when I completed filling it. Nothing, absolutely nothing, had changed in the condition of the ingredients. I had placed the urn at the end of a table in the reception hall and determined that, partway through dinner, I would plug it in to make an appropriately fresh pot for consumption with dessert. But the cord never got connected, and consequently, all of the perfectly placed, accurately measured, and correctly assembled pieces meant nothing. As James mentioned, "Faith by itself, if it does not have works, is dead" (James 2:17).

Throughout the preparation for the party, we assemble experiences, knowledge, resources, relationships and dreams. We can even have them in the proper place at the perfect time. But for our lives to be transformed, that's not enough. We need a connection to the power source, to the transforming agent.

In relationship with Christ, we become complete. We become a perfectly brewed cup of coffee for distribution, enjoyment, celebration, and warmth. Christ makes every ingredient in our lives come together in unity and significance.

We become what we were intended to become . . . complete, in and through Him, for the good purposes He planned for us before the foundation of the earth.

It's our choice: to be exactly as we had been . . . or be transformed.

His Wounds, Our Balm

Going a little farther he fell on his face and prayed, saying, "My Father, if it be possible, let this cup pass from me; nevertheless, not as I will, but as you will."

(MATTHEW 26:39)

I REMEMBER VIVIDLY THE days when our three children would struggle with a variety of illnesses. Often it was my job to coerce them into taking the appropriate medicine to help eliminate or dull the symptoms of their condition.

You know the tricks . . . distraction, bribes, intimidation . . . and a father's toolbox full of other methods. Every once in a while I would have to resort to the simple, direct, and pointed approach. It went something like this: "All right (Andrew, Erik, Alli), I know this medicine isn't fun to take, but you need to do this. It's for your own good. Trust Daddy." Compliance often was followed with a full body shiver as they choked down one more spoonful of hope.

In Matthew 26:39, we're privileged to be included in the intimate dialog between Jesus and the divine medicine giver. The remedy for the sins of mankind was the ultimate distasteful medicine. Jesus knew the bitterness of God's request. And so, much like any son or daughter would do, He asked His Father if there was any other way. Was there a hidden plan that could be revealed at the last minute . . . like God had miraculously done with Abraham and his son Isaac?

Yet in the midst of the anguished anticipation, Jesus defers. He was prepared to swallow the most painful medicine ever prescribed so that He could become our medicine. His sacrifice became our cure. His wounds, our balm.

I can only imagine the heart of the Father . . . looking into the pain-filled eyes of His only begotten Son. "Father, My Father . . . is there any other way? Is it really My task to embrace the sins of all mankind in My own sinless arms?" What pain for a father. And yet, for us . . . God looked into that face and said, "Trust Me."

God's prescription, our condition. Through Christ, we are healed.

THE COURAGE TO GO SLOW

Wait for the LORD; be strong, and let your heart take courage; wait for the LORD!

(PSALM 27:14)

MARY AND I HAVE TWICE ridden in the Elephant Rock bike ride. When we do so, we cover 100 kilometers. The course is rolling, and at points, challenging as we climb up and around the foothills of Colorado.

Because of some of the early and very steep hills on our route, it would be easy, at least for me, to completely exhaust myself before I'm a quarter of the way into the experience. This concern is well founded, given my tendency to compete and my compulsion to climb hills as fast as I can possibly push myself. This is just fine on a local twenty-mile ride, but it's clearly not a good strategy when I'm working to cover a much broader and expansive landscape.

While I have long understood that it takes discipline and at times courage to go fast, I now believe that in certain cases it takes an equal proportion of both to go slow. The conviction, and indeed the strategy, to go slow seems completely contrary to my nature on so many fronts. But frankly, it's necessary. In fact, a frantic pace is often both un-healthy and ineffective.

Jesus never operated at breakneck speed. You never read about Him racing to Galilee because He was late for an appointment. He didn't get frustrated with the traffic and the interruptions when He was on His way to heal a twelve-year-old girl in Mark 5. I don't believe that Jesus ever drove with His emergency flashers on. He had the courage and the discipline to go slow and submit to God's timing.

Had He not, He would have missed a transformational encounter with a woman who had spent twelve years racing from one possible medical solution to the next. Had He not, He might have moved past a group of children wanting a moment with Him. Had He not, He might have moved into an earlier trial and a premature end to His prophetic and historic call.

Waiting for God's timing, as the psalmist above suggests, takes courage. Do you have the courage to go slow? Not just for the practical reasons associated with a 62-mile bike ride, but in life . . . in living . . . in ministering and in being ministered to.

I'm convicted . . . and I'm convinced.

IN THE
SANCTUARY

When I thought how to understand this, it seemed to me a wearisome task,
until I went into the sanctuary of God; then I discerned their end.

(PSALM 73:16, 17)

IT WAS "IN THE sanctuary of God" that the psalmist found the answer to his honest and pressing questions. It was in the presence of the King that the turmoil over the prosperous enemies of God was settled . . . not in retribution or judgment, but simply by being in the presence of the Most High.

Perhaps this was on the heart of Jesus when He exposed His soul in Gethsemane, "My Father, if it be possible, let this cup pass from me; nevertheless, not as I will, but as you will" (Matthew 26:39).

Honesty oozes out of every syllable of the prayer. "If it is possible . . . another way, another strategy, another answer, a different payment." Jesus pleads at the deepest level with His Father. "Let this cup pass." And in doing so, in praying this prayer, He inspires every honest expression of pain and disappointment that I so often confine and contain within my soul.

Like the psalmist, Jesus strips the varnish off of the pain and exposes the raw grain of suffering. Then, with earth-rocking, love-infused faith, Jesus establishes a new level of trust and confidence. "Nevertheless . . ."

"Nevertheless" explodes from the sanctuary. Without a change in circumstance and while the enemy and the betrayer marched to the threshold of categoric defiance, Jesus lavishes obedient love upon His Father.

You . . . not me.

From the sanctuary . . . while in Gethsemane, hope erupts.

"My Father, if this cannot pass unless I drink it, Your will be done."

There was no problem with the faith of Jesus in this prayer. He didn't go to the cross because He didn't believe when He prayed. He went to the cross out of the deepest kind of faith.

Faith in God, His Father.

In the sanctuary . . . not my will, but Yours be done. Not in reluctant acquiescence, but in faith . . . the ultimate faith.

A DISTANT THUNDER

*From that time Jesus began to show his disciples that he must go to Jerusalem
and suffer many things from the elders and chief priests and scribes, and be killed,
and on the third day be raised.*

(MATTHEW 16:21)

THUNDER . . . in the distance. The rumble ushers in the anticipation. It warns us, in advance, of what's coming. Soon there will be the smell of rain, the flashes of lightning, the increased wind velocity. A storm is coming, and the warning invites preparation. Windows closed. Jacket in hand. Umbrella in briefcase. We're ready.

Jesus knew. His gruesome, painful, bloody death was known and anticipated. Although it looked like the act of an out of control vigilante uprising . . . it was the plan, the strategy, the mission. In Matthew 16, Jesus increases the volume of the thunder so that the disciples could hear. But it was more than they could comprehend. It was misguided worry. It was an overreaction to the political climate. It was an under appreciation of their ability to guard and protect.

Yes, Jesus knew. He knew all along. The price for Him to absorb our penalty was substantial. When He left His Father's side to make Himself nothing (Philippians 2:7), He knew the cost.

The rumble, now closer, caused no panic, no "two-minute offense," no marketing blitz, no self-pity. Humility, sacrifice, substitution, and rejection were the design. They had to be, for the sake of justice, for the purity of the Father, for the ransom that was due.

And as He moved toward the cross, Jesus not only modeled sacrifice, but He taught us to incline our ears as well . . . to listen for the thunder. To hear what others do not. To respond with resolve, with sacrifice, with mercy, with love.

Everywhere. In every neighborhood. In an urban ghetto and in the shell-shocked boardrooms across this country . . . fear has replaced self-reliance. Thunder.

The time is now "to do justice, and to love kindness, and to walk humbly with your God" (Micah 6:8).

The cross shows us the way. It was the strategy. The victory was costly . . . but calculated. Jesus taught us to anticipate. To serve. To sacrifice. To comfort and to confront . . . without panic. To grasp with confidence the sovereign hand of God.

Thunder. . . . it is the sound of sacrifice. The invitation to intercede.

It is time for the followers of Jesus to show the way, to be the Church, to fulfill our call.

Listen . . . do you hear the thunder?

THE TOUCH
OF LOVE

*There came a man full of leprosy. And when he saw Jesus, he fell on his face and
begged him, "Lord, if you will, you can make me clean." And Jesus stretched out his
hand and touched him, saying, "I will; be clean."*

(LUKE 5:12, 13)

*The leprous person who has the disease shall wear torn clothes and let the hair of his
head hang loose, and he shall cover his upper lip and cry out, "Unclean, unclean." He
shall remain unclean as long as he has the disease. He is unclean. He shall live alone.
His dwelling shall be outside the camp.*

(LEVITICUS 13:45, 46)

This was the law. This was the destiny for leprous citizens.
Unclean. Alone. Outcast.

This is what makes the encounter of Jesus in Luke 5 so bold and
courageous.

There was no mistaken identity, for this man was "full of leprosy."
And as he approached Jesus, there was a decision to be made—a decision that crossed the lines of justice and invaded the space of mercy
and grace.

I have no doubt that Jesus could have simply spoken the word and
healing would have invaded every corner and every cell of this man;
but healing was only part of the lesson that Jesus wanted to teach.
"And Jesus stretched out his hand and touched him."

Unclean became clean; broken became whole. And as it did, Jesus
shattered the boundaries of prejudice, bias, arrogance, and shame.

Jesus wasted no time in diagnosis. He knew exactly what He was dealing with. And as He stretched out His hand, He obliterated every argument that we could use to insulate ourselves from the outcast and disposed.

"He is unclean. He shall live alone." The disease and the sentence had met their match, but more importantly, the victim had met the Savior. There was nothing clinical about the solution. No latex cloths. No delegation of duties. It was an assault . . . with a touch. Perfect skin on diseased skin.

This was no aberration or tangent in the ministry life of Jesus. This was a full-on endorsement and example of love in action. Jesus touched what others despised. He will never ignore the pain, grief, loneliness, or ugliness. This is the message of Jesus, and it underscores the way of life that He expects from His followers.

"I will," said Jesus.

Will we?

COME TO JESUS

Come to me, all who labor and are heavy laden, and I will give you rest.

(MATTHEW 11:28)

A FEW YEARS AGO I stood in the lobby of the corporate office of the technology giant Google. I was there to discuss a potential business partnership, but while I waited for the individual I was to meet with, I watched a large screen monitor that hung above the reception desk. The screen revealed the current Google searches that were being requested from around the world . . . I'm sure with some filtering technology applied.

It was fascinating to watch the pleas for help from all across the world. I saw names, questions, phrases, and a variety of other expressions . . . all with a singular motivation and cry: "Can you help me?"

Google is a safe and reliable source. No judgment cast, no requirements—just pages of options in milliseconds.

Millions of questions every day. Yet what about life's most important questions? What about the keys to significance and meaning? Where's the search engine for the core elements of living?

Jesus had an answer . . .

Are you tired? Worn out? Burned out on religion? Come to me. Get away with me and you'll recover your life. I'll show you how to take a real rest. Walk with me and work with me—watch how I do it. Learn the unforced rhythms of grace. I won't lay anything heavy or ill-fitting on you. Keep company with me and you'll learn to live freely and lightly.

(MATTHEW 11:28-30, MSG)

There it is. "Come to me." That's what Jesus said, and what He meant.

Jesus says, "I'm not afraid of the deepest search in your life. Your pursuit of meaning and significance doesn't overwhelm Me. Bring Me your brokenness, your failure, your hurt, your pain. I won't mock you, reject you, or dismiss you; after all, I've heard them all! Come to Me with your questions and I'll give you the only answer that matters."

He's safe and reliable. Are you searching? Are you out of options? Are you tired of looking everywhere else? Come to Him.

He is the answer to the most profound search in life.

Authentic questions . . . the real answer.

Power unleashed. In milliseconds.

THE MASTER'S NOD

For we do not have a high priest who is unable to sympathize with our weaknesses, but one who in every respect has been tempted as we are, yet without sin. Let us then with confidence draw near to the throne of grace, that we may receive mercy and find grace to help in time of need.

(HEBREWS 4:15, 16)

MY ONE REAL EXERCISE passion is road biking. Consequently, my family's move to Denver was great at feeding this desire. The paved trails that crisscross the city are outstanding. Specifically, the South Platte River Trail is a favorite. It snakes along with the flow of the river all the way to downtown.

The path is used extensively. In fact, over much of the distance there is actually a painted center line to organize traffic. This is a path for serious cyclists, which consequently makes me feel like I fit, even though the jury is still out on that subject.

What I've come to discover is the "language" of cyclists. As you encounter fully-decked, wonderfully-equipped riders along the path, you use the cyclist's greeting. From my experience, that's simply a quickly connected glance and an equally quick nod of the head. It's the head nod that's the big deal. It's like sign language for cyclists. In that single gesture is acknowledgment, validation, and encouragement. With the single click of the head, there is hope. It conveys this message: "I've been where you're going." Sometimes the riders look exhausted and weathered, but the message is reassuring nonetheless: "I did it!"

Did you catch it? The divine head nod. The cyclist greeting at a celestial level. It's Jesus, catching a quick connecting glance with His children. He tips His head forward in greeting and reassurance. "I've been where you're going" is exactly what He conveys.

Yes, I'm flooded with hope. Indeed, He did it.

Whatever it is . . . doubt, fear, pain, frustration, disobedience . . . Jesus has charted the path to holiness. Join the Overcomer. Accept the nod from the Master Cyclist with confidence . . . because of Jesus.

THE ULTIMATE
EXCHANGE

Behold, a woman of the city, who was a sinner, when she learned that he was reclining at table in the Pharisee's house, brought an alabaster flask of ointment, and standing behind him at his feet, weeping, she began to wet his feet with her tears and wiped them with the hair of her head and kissed his feet and anointed them with the ointment. . . . And he said to her, "Your sins are forgiven."

(LUKE 7:37, 38, 48)

WEDNESDAY WAS TOWEL EXCHANGE day at Crooked Creek camp in Frasier, Colorado. Four hundred and twenty-five campers were encouraged to meet at the center circle of camp and trade the towel and wash cloth that they had been using for three days for clean, dry and neatly-folded replacements.

As high school students meandered out of their various cabins on their way to the circle, I couldn't help but reflect on the symmetry of the moment.

Our theme for Wednesday at camp was "Jesus Sees My Mess." And the invitation to vulnerability had exposed more pain, anger, despair, and bitterness than I thought could ever be accumulated in the relatively short lives of the campers.

Lives lived in the shadow of shame, guilt, addiction, and loneliness have produced an explosion of pain that breaks even the toughest heart. But that night, in the stillness of a summer evening in the mountains of Colorado, we described the offer of a lifetime: the ultimate exchange. My sorrows, my shame, my pain, my secrets and the poison that accompanies them exchanged for the unconditional and transformational love of God our Father.

Tears flowed. Pain subsided. Hope returned as one by one, young people came to terms with an exchange of cosmic, yet deeply personal, proportions.

Yes, Jesus understands. Sinners are redeemed; the broken restored. I'm humbled to witness God at work.

The ultimate exchange. Our dirt, our rags for His cleansing power. It happened in the mountains of Colorado. Has it happened for you?

KINGDOM GREATNESS

Whoever receives one such child in my name receives me, and whoever receives me, receives not me but him who sent me.

(MARK 9:37)

THE POLLS WERE STILL open, the commentators were still speculating and the candidates were debating their positions with intensity and passion. They had spent enough time with the incumbent to mimic a portion of His behavior and lifestyle. It was simply the right moment to discuss placement. Who was leading the pack? Who had most effectively embraced the recipe for success?

Jesus interrupted the posturing with the skill of a surgeon slicing through an obstacle. "What were you discussing on the way?" (Mark 9:33). The answer stuck in the disciples' throat as embarrassment washed over them. Jesus didn't wait for a reply . . . He knew the answer as clearly as they did. On their hike to Capernaum they had been transfixed on the subject of greatness, and more specifically, which of them was emerging as the favorite.

Without an overt rebuke, Jesus opened His figurative dictionary and thumbed to the page on Kingdom greatness. He used words like *last* and *servant* to describe front-runner status.

Then with precision and impeccable timing, He placed a child in the center of their pompous discussion and within a few moments He had scooped the child into His arms. The tenderness and focus of His action breathed life into His words. "Whoever receives one such child in my name receives me, and whoever receives me, receives not me but him who sent me" (Mark 9:37).

Jesus didn't chastise their desire to be "the greatest"; He simply put a job description in front of their application.

In doing so, He spoke into the lives of every one of His followers. He inverted the corporate ladder, He flipped the pyramid of success and obliterated the strategy of self-promotion. Jesus didn't dismantle the metal stand. Instead, He shed light on what a top performer would do . . . and, more importantly, on why he or she would do it.

With this encounter, Jesus positioned every individual that we are tempted to ignore squarely in our path. He highlighted what we would typically erase. He valued what we would generally round off.

Today, within a few minutes of reading this, you'll have the opportunity to live what Jesus defined. There will be a child in your midst, and you'll have a decision to make.

Keep your Kingdom dictionary close. Embrace the insignificant. Welcome the outsider. Serve. For when you do, you are receiving God Himself.

The polls are still open indeed.

THE KEYS TO THE KINGDOM

I will give you the keys of the kingdom of heaven, and whatever you bind on earth shall be bound in heaven, and whatever you loose on earth shall be loosed in heaven.

(MATTHEW 16:19)

THE OTHER DAY, IN the course of racing from a conference call to an appointment, I found myself digging in my pocket for the keys that would give me access to a rental car and a hotel room. When I arrived at an office complex where I had a meeting, a bar-coded name badge gave me the necessary electronic permission to avail myself of a bank of elevators that took me to the nineteenth floor.

Keys open possibilities and they restrict them. They launch, ignite, and extinguish. They unlock and they prevent. Keys grant authority . . . they mysteriously open and close.

A plastic card, an oddly shaped electronic fob, an elegantly crafted antique skeleton key . . . all have purpose. Access. Control. Power. Strength.

In the waning moments of Jesus' earthly ministry, He placed the keys of the "kingdom of heaven" in the palm of Peter's calloused hand. In the days ahead, they would bounce around in his heart like a single key in a bottomless pocket. He would fiddle with them, misplace them, try and force them into the wrong lock. But ultimately and confidently, he would slide them into the lock and he would masterfully release the gospel to a crowd of listeners in Acts 2. "And I will show wonders in the heavens above and signs on the earth below," he would declare, because he had the keys (2:19). "Everyone who calls upon the name of the Lord shall be saved," he would add, because he had witnessed firsthand the power of the gospel (2:21).

> *So those who received his word were baptized, and there were added that day about three thousand souls.*

> (Acts 2:41)

The keys to the kingdom of heaven: unlocking an explosion of God's power through the release of the Good News.

> *The Lord sets the prisoners free.*

> (Psalm 146:7)

He frees captives and prisoners with the only key that fits the lock: God's Good News—the Message of hope; the formula for freedom. Keys . . . now in the palm of our hand.

NO TERROR
IN LOVE

You have heard that it was said, "You shall love your neighbor and hate your enemy."
But I say to you, Love your enemies and pray for those who persecute you.

(MATTHEW 5:43, 44)

ONE WEEKEND AS I sat and watched several unfolding news stories, I was drawn to the continual, and in some cases, escalating violence in Iraq. Like you, I viewed the images with disbelief and horror. The pictures included those of vehicles that look like automotive skeletons and of people who weep and wail for the lives snuffed out by the senseless acts of violence. The rationale for such acts is "sectarian." In other words, deep-seated religious belief systems that find noncompliant belief systems, and consequently carve a path of collision.

Such commitment to a cause forced me to ask a question . . . Am I less committed than these terrorists? Is the Christian community generally less brave, less passionate, and less sold out for the truth it embraces?

Later, while I was spending time reflecting on the tenets of the faith as defined in Scripture, I discovered the answer in Matthew 5:43, 44. Being sold out for the Christian faith takes me/us to a radically different destination. It's a place that is no less demanding.

The intersection of belief systems for Christians takes us to a place of love, not violence. It compels us to intercede, not retaliate. The motivation is not tolerance, but compassion. The reference point for this behavior is not weakness, but rather a common need for grace and mercy.

Christianity needs no car bombs to defend it. In fact, the very tools of the faith dismantle hatred. The followers of Christ demonstrate ultimate courage by resisting the urge to lash out, not because they can't, but because they won't.

And behold, one of those who were with Jesus stretched out his hand and drew his sword and struck the servant of the high priest and cut off his ear. Then Jesus said to him, "Put your sword back into its place. For all who take the sword will perish by the sword. Do you think that I cannot appeal to my Father, and he will at once send me more than twelve legions of angels?"

(Matthew 26:51-53)

There is no terror in love. It defuses what hatred ignites.
A higher standard—confident in truth, compassionate in defense.

COUNT IT
ALL JOY

*Count it all joy, my brothers, when you meet trials of various kinds, for you know that
the testing of your faith produces steadfastness. And let steadfastness have its full effect,
that you may be perfect and complete, lacking in nothing.*

(JAMES 1:2-4)

I WAS FOUR MILES from help when I had my first flat tire on my
road bike. I had no spare parts and no tools to even attempt to repair
the damage. So I walked and pushed until a kind-hearted older man
came to my rescue. That very day I purchased a tire repair kit that I
placed in a small pouch under the seat of my bike.

That was several years ago, and since that experience I've had more
than twenty times to practice what I learned. I can't explain it. So
instead of explanations, I've gotten really good at repairing and replac-
ing my bike tube. I not only carry repair equipment, but also a replace-
ment tube, a special CO_2 canister for rapid inflation, and an additional
hand pump.

What immobilized me several years ago has now become a well-
practiced routine. I'm ready in attitude, equipment and confidence.
Don't get me wrong, I'm still not crazy about flat tires, but I'm no
longer controlled by them. Preparation and practice have transformed
a road block into a speed bump.

For the first few years of my road-biking exploits, I ignored the
possibility. I convinced myself that flats happened to careless people.
"They probably had it coming," I would tell myself. "They must have
done something wrong, or they must not be doing something right."

My arrogance fueled my ignorance, and with it a false sense of righteousness and safety. But a few years ago that changed.

I'm more humble today. I know that flats happen, even when I'm not careless or stupid. Sometimes there are thorns or spurs along the trail that I simply can't see. The only way to avoid them is to avoid riding altogether . . . and that wouldn't solve anything.

So turn me loose. I'm not only ready to ride, I'm ready to persevere. I'm not just okay when the tires are full; I know what to do when they're not. And most importantly, I'm ready to help other people. People with flat tires. People who ran into problems simply because they rode the path.

No longer immobilized. No longer prone to condemn. Flat tires and still "counting it all joy."

PROVE IT!

*Prove by the way you live that you have repented of your sins
and turned to God.*

(LUKE 3:8, NLT)

HAVE YOU EVER MET anyone like John the Baptist? Sold out.
Unleashed. Zealous. It's no wonder that when John began to preach,
his messages were pointed and inspired; after all, he was appointed by
God to be the igniter for the light of the world.

John never softened his messages to draw a crowd. On the contrary,
he consistently upped the ante on what it meant to be a God follower.
The words above were spoken to a group of pretenders—religious
wannabes.

"Prove it! Show everyone who knows you that you've had an encounter with the living God. Reveal your new identity by the mark of
your behavior."

"What should we do?" was the follow-up question from the convicted group of listeners.

John's answer stung: "If you have two shirts, give one to the poor. If
you have food, share it with those who are hungry" (3:11, NLT).

*Even corrupt tax collectors came to be baptized and asked, "Teacher, what should we
do?" He replied, "Collect no more taxes than the government requires."
"What should we do?" asked some soldiers. John replied, "Don't extort money or
make false accusations. And be content with your pay."*

(LUKE 3:12-14, NLT)

If John the Baptist were alive today . . . if you had him over for dinner . . . if you grabbed a bagel and a skinny latté, what would he say?

I don't know about you, but I have some work to do. By God's grace and in His power, let's live the call of the Baptizer!

HIS COMPASSION

When he saw the crowds, he had compassion for them, because they were harassed and helpless, like sheep without a shepherd.

(Matthew 9:36)

COMPASSION IS INCONVENIENT AND often intrusive. It lays claim to our attention and engages our heart. It suggests, in unavoidable terms, that we get involved. It climbs the sharp cliffs of selflessness.

This is the pattern of Jesus, and it was often demonstrated at the pinnacle of demand—when Jesus was the most obliged to thoughts of convenience. He returned the volley of an inquisitive and needy throng with personal, specific, and sacrificial involvement.

Touched by a hemorrhaging woman, He engaged . . . (Matthew 9).

Confronted by a leprous man, He touched . . . (Matthew 8).

Interrupted while preaching, He commended and then healed . . . (Mark 2).

During the most intense ministry schedule, He empathized . . . (Matthew 9).

Without solicitation, He got involved . . . (Luke 7).

In the face of opposition, He risked . . . (John 5).

Followed by a hungry wave of groupies, He welcomed, and fed . . . (Luke 9).

And yes, Jesus always blended His compassion with liberal doses of grace and truth. He offered healing and hope and sympathy and solutions both temporal and eternal.

So now you understand the pain in my soul when I walked into the Anaheim Convention Center where roughly 6,000 students and adults gathered to hear the compassionate and transformational message of Jesus as part of our DCLA 2006 conference . . . and I encountered a small group of individuals holding signs and confronting young people with caustic and confrontational words. Under the banner of Christianity, these individuals chastised, condemned, and criticized. Compassion, even for young people, was displaced by argument and debate. It was venomous, but it was isolated, and moments later it was overcome by the power of God's Word and the living reality of His compassion.

I was there when all around the massive convention center, broken, wounded, lonely, and desperate individuals stood to their feet in an honest plea for help. I was there when compassion ruled. I was there when mercy won. I was there when grace flourished.

May we be like Jesus.

GET TO
KNOW HIM

Inasmuch as many have undertaken to compile a narrative of the things that have been accomplished among us, just as those who from the beginning were eyewitnesses and ministers of the word have delivered them to us, it seemed good to me also, having followed all things closely for some time past, to write an orderly account for you, most excellent Theophilus, that you may have certainty concerning the things you have been taught.

(LUKE 1:1-4)

I RECEIVED A MOLESKINE for Christmas. It's a black notebook that is manufactured by an Italian company with the same name. It is distinct because of the elastic band that keeps the notebook closed and the binding that enables it to lay flat. Basically, my kids tell me that it's the coolest journal out there. That's enough for me.

Just receiving the gift has motivated me to keep an orderly account of my year. I have pages set aside for noting exercise activity. Another section is devoted to highlighting the books that I will be reading this year. And, of course, there is the daily record of the activities and impressions that experientially inform my life.

Do you suppose that this was the way that Dr. Luke felt when he started his Gospel with the words above?

Luke addresses this Gospel account to a friend and student. To confirm in the heart and mind of Theophilus "the things you have been taught." So Luke decided that the most effective way to do this was with an orderly account: a "moleskinesque" kind of journal that captured the activity and the corresponding impact of the life of Jesus . . . the Christ.

Perhaps this is why Luke starts with the human life of Christ at its earliest phase. Perhaps this is why Luke invites us into the doubt of Zechariah, into the exhilaration of Elizabeth, into the ponderous and promising heart of Mary. Perhaps this is why we have the opportunity to peek into the journal of the shepherds, and Simeon and Anna in the temple. For this reason we see the inquisitive heart of a twelve-year-old Jesus who was as captivated by the discourse of the temple teachers as twelve-year-olds are today with the Nintendo Wii.

Yes, Luke embarked on an orderly account, and so will I. Will you join me on an orderly, Moleskine-like pursuit . . . to know Jesus more intimately, more intensely, more tenderly, and more powerfully?

BE A BLIZZARD

On this rock I will build my church, and the gates of hell shall not prevail against it.

(MATTHEW 16:18)

THE SEMI-TRUCKS WERE LINED up poised, positioned, and powerless. Most of the rigs were loaded with thousands of pounds of cargo. The powerful diesel engines idled, but without effect. The white flags of submission were out.

An examination of the situation revealed that their conqueror was a tiny crystal of frozen water, more commonly known as a snowflake. As absurd as it sounds, it was true. I witnessed it firsthand. The transportation corridor between Kansas and Colorado, better known as Interstate 70, was closed. Nothing, not a van with our family of seven, not an elaborate traction-rich vehicle, and not even an eighty-thousand-pound semi-truck could defeat what had accumulated in six hours. Game over!

It's incredible that something so insignificant, so invisible, could overwhelm and disable such a powerful infrastructure. But we all know, snow doesn't fall in isolation. One snowflake introduces another. And every once in a while, a countless number fall at the same time and when this concert of nature is accompanied by a powerful and artistic wind, the work becomes a blizzard. And then roads, even interstates, close.

I'm convinced that Jesus understood this phenomenon at another level. He called it the Church. Millions of individuals, often insignificant, come together with a common mission and vision. They know that there is power when they come together in pristine unity. They know that when they offer themselves, fully, completely, sacrificially, collectively, and the powerful wind of the Spirit blows, that nothing, absolutely nothing, can overpower it.

No march of evil. No engine of hate. No scheme of destruction.

These categoric words of Jesus were a forecast and a promise. A blizzard is coming. Snowflakes. One at a time. Commonly purposed. Spirit driven. The Church.

Not even the gates of hell. Let's be what Jesus declared that we should be. Let's be The Church. Let's be a blizzard.

When the snow falls, and the Wind blows . . . revival, real, infrastructure-changing revival comes.

LISTEN

Jesus took with him Peter and James and John, and led them up a high mountain
by themselves. And he was transfigured before them, and his clothes became radiant,
intensely white, as no one on earth could bleach them. And there appeared to them
Elijah with Moses, and they were talking with Jesus. And Peter said to Jesus, "Rabbi,
it is good that we are here. Let us make three tents, one for you and one for Moses and
one for Elijah." For he did not know what to say, for they were terrified.

(MARK 9:2-6)

OFTEN, AFTER AN EXPERIENCE of deep connection with the
Father, on the heels of a poignant and sacred encounter, we want to
race to action. The combustion in our soul fuels a desire to engage in
activity.

Like Peter, we want to grab our toolbox and build a tent . . . maybe
three! Peter, in the midst of an awesome moment, during a momentary lapse in the divine conversation, fills the gap with the suggestion
that he and his buddies get busy building something.

And the response to Peter's poorly-framed idea comes from God!
Not from angels, not from the Old Testament prophets . . . not even
from Jesus. Peter's fumbling, mindless lob is returned with an answer
from God: "And a cloud overshadowed them, and a voice came out of
the cloud, 'This is my beloved Son; listen to him'" (Mark 9:7).

"Listen to him." Don't talk, don't build, don't memorialize, don't
mobilize armies, don't launch campaigns, don't do. *Listen.*

The tendency of the human heart is to fill the womb of pregnant
moments with activity. We construct when we should contemplate.
We pound nails when we should ponder.

But God has different ideas . . . on the mountaintop, and in the
valley.

Listen.

Listen to Him.

Listen to His beloved, compassionate, powerful, tender, awesome, miraculous, humble, gentle, committed, sacrificial Son . . . our Savior.

Listen to Him.

Welcoming a Child

And they were bringing children to him that he might touch them, and the disciples rebuked them. But when Jesus saw it, he was indignant and said to them, "Let the children come to me; do not hinder them, for to such belongs the kingdom of God. Truly, I say to you, whoever does not receive the kingdom of God like a child shall not enter it." And he took them in his arms and blessed them, laying his hands on them.

(MARK 10:13-16)

ONE MORNING I WAS on a very early Southwest flight out of Denver, and fortunately, I was in the "A" line for seat selection. This is critical to ensure an appropriate aisle seat with adequate overhead bin space. A small group of "pre-boards" had filed into the Boeing 737 and it was now my turn to walk the aisle, evaluate the situation, and to process the available options . . . selecting the one that most appropriately suited my requirements for the two hours to Chicago Midway Airport.

The criteria is simple: an aisle seat as far forward as possible. *Perfect,* I thought. *Lots of options available.* I looked at a completely vacant

row 6, a partially vacant row 7, tossed my suitcase above, and quickly
surveyed the landscape one more time. It was then that my eyes
caught a family in row 8. A mother in the window seat, a baby in
her lap, and her small child in the middle seat. At the same time that
my internal warning flags went up, "Clear the area! Clear the area!"
so did a powerful and irresistible urge to simply drop into the seat
next to the four-year-old girl. And I did just that. I quickly glanced
back through the plane and realized that I had just done something
completely illogical, especially for me. I had invited interruption, but I
couldn't move. I didn't want to move.

Instantly, Zion introduced herself. She talked with familiarity,
warmth, and abandon. I would periodically glance at her mother to
invite interpretation of the unmistakable childish babble, but sponta-
neously a friendship was born.

I heard about a Daddy in the Army, Nana in Chicago, baby sister,
Zena, napping in her mother's arms. I had a play-by-play of the apple
juice in her glass. And yes, even without a word, her eyes welcomed
my engagement, my interest, my seat selection.

Two hours later, Zion asked me if I would come to her birthday
party . . . it was only eleven months away. She must know my schedule,
and I probably should have given her June Thompson's email address .
. . because this little girl did something for me.

She was disarming, bold, unafraid, and sweet. The few moments I
did catch an airplane nap, I woke to a pair of deep brown eyes peering
into my face, into my soul.

I was reading through the four Gospels that month. Mid-flight
from Denver to Chicago, I journeyed through Mark 10.

Enough said.

131

An Eternal Investment

Do not lay up for yourselves treasures on earth, where moth and rust destroy and where thieves break in and steal, but lay up for yourselves treasures in heaven, where neither moth nor rust destroys and where thieves do not break in and steal. For where your treasure is, there your heart will be also.

(Matthew 6:19-21)

WE WERE ON OUR way to New York's LaGuardia Airport. Few times in my flying experience have I been in a more turbulent environment. These were not quaint little bumps and rolls;, they were mid-air potholes that left passengers gasping.

I had a headset on with channel 9 selected. This enabled me to listen to the air traffic controller and the dialog with a variety of airplanes that he was tasked with bringing into the airport. I listened carefully to every instruction for United flight 640.

On final approach, the air traffic controller instructed our flight crew to abandon our landing attempt and divert immediately to Kennedy International Airport roughly twenty minutes away.

The chatter from Kennedy Airport was even more intense as a number of diverted aircraft raced to outrun the tremendous mid-summer thunderstorm. Again on final approach, I heard the dialog between the pilots and the control tower. Within a few minutes, a flight in front of ours on the runway reported wind shear, one of the most dangerous phenomenon that pilots face. The pilot noted that he encountered the condition at 650 feet and didn't recover control until 300 feet.

The tower repeated the message: "United 640, wind shear was reported at 650 feet." Our pilot confirmed, but continued. Instantly our plane was introduced to new levels of turbulence and the anxiety in the cabin was unmistakable. Mary sat beside me, eyes closed, feigning sleep, but practicing prayer. I listened and waited.

At the pinnacle of one of the most frightening flights of my life, I felt a peace that was as unmistakable as the thrashing. Once the wheels were rolling on pavement and the passengers had exploded in spontaneous applause, Mary looked at me and said, "Wow, you were really calm." And she was right.

In those moments of uncertainty, even while listening to the details surrounding the turbulent situation, I knew, really knew, that my treasure in heaven was something that moth, rust, thieves, wind shear, thunderstorms, and devastation couldn't destroy. In that moment I knew a peace that indeed passed understanding (Philippians 4:7).

On that mountainside in Galilee, Jesus knew what we would face. He knew what we would anchor our hopes in, what would distract us from His hope. So He gave us a plan: Invest in eternity and the turbulence won't matter.

Now I understand.

WHO DO YOU SAY THAT HE IS?

And he asked them, "But who do you say that I am?" Peter answered him, "You are the Christ." And he strictly charged them to tell no one about him. And he began to teach them that the Son of Man must suffer many things and be rejected by the elders and the chief priests and the scribes and be killed, and after three days rise again. . . . Peter took him aside and began to rebuke him.

(MARK 8:29-32)

PETER, WHO DECLARES THAT Jesus is the Son of the living God, now exposes the depth of his own agenda, and his own miscalculation of the immensity of the chasm between God and man.

Peter's blunder is recorded for all of us to inspect . . . and as such, he exposes the unfortunate tendencies in my own life. This is the tendency to waste my time trying to figure out what God will, or should, do next. While Peter is getting ready to go to Home Depot to select the wood for Jesus' throne, our Lord is captured by the significance of the impending cross. While Peter is wondering where he'll fit in the class roster, particularly since he seemed to get an A+ on his last exam, Jesus is emptying Himself.

Over and over the Lord reminds me that those who want to be first have to be prepared to be last. That whoever wants to save his life will lose it, but whoever loses his life for Christ's sake will find it.

From the head of the class, straight to detention. This is harsh, but true. Sin is costly, and Jesus, the Son of the living God stepped into the vortex of God's justice for us, for the sake of love, in obedience to His Father.

Peter, our brother, stepped squarely into the dung heap of self-confidence and in so doing he exposes the stench of pride that swirls in my own walk with Jesus. It is the faithful that Jesus commends . . . not those who "figure Him out." There is no puzzle to be completed; there is sin to pay for. By God's grace, Jesus did just that. He is indeed, the Son of the living God, our Savior.

Who do you say that He is?

LOVING
JESUS-STYLE

I say to you, Love your enemies and pray for those who persecute you. . . .
For if you love those who love you, what reward do you have?
Do not even the tax collectors do the same?

(MATTHEW 5:44, 46)

I LOVE MY FRIENDS. In fact, one weekend recently I spent time with some of my closest and most faithful friends . . . many of whom are family as well. These individuals are loyal, wise, and trusted. They know my weaknesses and strengths. They know how to pick me up when I'm down, and how to celebrate with me as well. It is a treasure to have them as a part of my life.

As Jesus approached the halfway point in His most profound sermon, He started to drastically up the stakes for those who desired to follow Him. In doing so, He called His followers to distinguish themselves in powerful and provocative ways.

One portion of that discourse focused on those that I love . . . you know, the very people that I just described. Jesus doesn't discount or discourage my love for these important people in my life; He simply puts this love in context.

Real love, Jesus-style love, expands the breadth of love. It understands that embracing and being embraced by those I find easily lovable is only the preface to a landmark classic on love.

So Jesus does what Jesus alone can do . . . He raises the bar to levels only achievable when He is firmly in the mix. His admonition comes in the first verse above. And He delivered this word just moments after He had sucked the life out of the human tendency to retaliate: "If anyone slaps you on the right cheek, turn to him the other also"; "let him have your cloak as well"; "go with him two miles" (5:39-41).

And so Jesus does it again. He sets a standard that defies the inclination of my soul, and in doing so He proclaims: "With God all things are possible" (19:26).

The life of Jesus reflected and resolved the disconnects of our human nature with our divine appointments. Jesus did it, and He instructed us to follow His lead.

And so we pray for, sacrifice for, work for, weep over, laugh with our enemies. When we do, we show the world what Jesus is all about.

FISHERS OF MEN

"Follow me, and I will make you fishers of men."
Immediately they left their nets and followed him.

(MATTHEW 4:19, 20)

ON A RECENT VACATION, I loaded bikes, suitcases, and food into our van to head to Wyoming for a week of rest, family interaction . . . and yes, fishing. To be clear, I am not a fisherman. I appreciate the sport and the corresponding challenges associated with attracting and "capturing" an elusive target.

So with eight inexperienced adults headed to the North Platte River . . . it was clear that we needed help. We hoped for careful, insightful, and patient support and teaching in order to lure beautiful trout. Our hosts, Larry and Margo Bean, made certain that we had great guides to accompany and mentor us along the adventure.

When Jesus transitioned from the language of fishing to the corresponding language of ministry as He talked with His disciples, He did so with the commitment of guidance. He traversed the white water of their uncertainty and, as He did so, He promised to show them the way to effectively and authentically build transformational relationships with those who need to know the Father.

He promised to make them fishers of men.

Patiently, thoughtfully, powerfully . . . Jesus took three years to demonstrate the lifestyle of compassion, care, discipline, solitude, study, prayer, humility, and love so that He could engage effectively in His Father's mission . . . to seek and save the lost (Luke 19:10).

Jesus was the ultimate fishing guide. "Follow me" was His invitation. Three years later His disciples were ready.

Now when they heard this they were cut to the heart, and said to Peter and the rest of the apostles, "Brothers, what shall we do?" And Peter said to them, "Repent and be baptized every one of you in the name of Jesus Christ for the forgiveness of your sins, and you will receive the gift of the Holy Spirit. For the promise is for you and for your children and for all who are far off, everyone whom the Lord our God calls to himself."

(ACTS 2:37-39)

Jesus ... the perfect fishing guide. Follow Him.

A PLEA FOR MORE

"Do you see anything?" And he looked up and said, "I see men,
but they look like trees, walking."

(MARK 8:23, 24)

UH-OH. JESUS' ENCOUNTER WITH the blind man at Bethsaida looks an awful lot like His supernatural power misfired. Either He underestimated the force of the defect, or He misappropriated His healing power. In either case, when Jesus asked the blind man to take a quick glance at the eye chart after He had applied His healing balm, He got a "less than satisfactory" on the report.

Was this a divine foul ball? Had the sheer exhaustion from the pace of feeding thousands, dialoging with skeptics, teaching, mentoring, and healing finally caught up with Him? Was He out of juice, underpowered, overtaxed or unprepared?

Not a chance! Jesus, God's Son, spoke every word and delivered every action with the precise purposes and plans of God as His guide. A multi-phased healing process was not a "two-swings at bat" in the game of life.

Masterfully, Jesus used this healing experience as a metaphor for life and learning.

What if this blind man, exposed to a world of darkness, had been prepared to live with the vast improvement of imperfect sight? What if he had stopped wanting more? For undoubtedly, seeing men that look like trees walking is a quantum leap over the chasm of nothing. Yet his honesty became his petition, and the response of Christ became a megaphone to the body and the soul.

More of Christ. More of His healing power. More drink for the thirsty, more healing for the broken, more forgiveness for the shamed, more love for the bitter, more tenderness for the rigid, more holiness for the sinner. Just more of Jesus.

What if the prayer of my soul was an acknowledgement of the progress and a plea for more? What if our prayers echoed the heartbeat of the father of the boy in Mark 9:24 who pled, "I believe; help my unbelief"?

What if our bodies and souls clamored for more . . . not in disrespect but in expectation; not with dissatisfaction but with anticipation?

> *Then Jesus laid his hands on his eyes again; and he opened his eyes,*
> *his sight was restored, and he saw everything clearly.*

(MARK 8:25)

Our hunger for more becomes His banquet table. Our thirst invites His wellspring.

More of Jesus . . . I want more.

THE MASTER
TEACHER

*Seeing the crowds, he went up on the mountain, and when he sat down, his disciples
came to him. And he opened his mouth and taught them.*

(MATTHEW 5:1, 2)

IT WAS MARCH OF 2000 in Crotonville, New York and I was part
of a General Electric training course. This was a full three-week inten-
sive with no time away for good behavior. The curriculum anchored
the sixty students in a strong business understanding, with some of
the finest instructors in the world.

As the end of our educational foray neared, we were informed that
the President of GE would be taking an afternoon to meet with us.
Jack Welch was an icon in GE circles, and a personal, interactive, and
lengthy visit by him was the payoff that many had hoped for.

When Jack stepped to the front of the Crotonville classroom, silence, anticipation, and focus swept across the room. We were there to
be taught, listen, scribe, and engage when asked. This was the classroom of the master, a forum to learn the lessons of a man who had
grown a company into a $300 billion corporate juggernaut.

There were no slick leather chairs or high-tech setups in Jesus'
classroom—just a sloped terrain and outdoor aesthetics. He didn't
need amplification or glossy brochures. Yet when He gathered His ad
hoc class around Him, the message reverberated throughout history.
It was edgy, provocative, and powerful. It was heavily seasoned with
compassion and love. To this day the lessons remain relevant and
profound.

There was no corporate behemoth birthed on that slope . . . just the most powerful living movement that mankind has ever known: the Church! And nothing, not a Wall Street meltdown, the horror of a terrorist attack, or the fear of a potential executive scandal can disrupt the trajectory of God's plan for His people.

The most powerful sermon ever preached ripped through religion, politics, economics, relationships, desperation, and fear. The wave still hasn't hit shore.

The Master Teacher. The living Lord. Our Savior.

It was Calvary, not Crotonville, that changed my life.

ONE OF
THOSE DAYS

On one of those days, as he was teaching, Pharisees and teachers of the law were sitting
there, who had come from every village of Galilee and Judea and from Jerusalem.
And the power of the Lord was with him to heal.

(LUKE 5:17)

HAVE YOU EVER HAD "one of those days"? It strikes me that
Dr. Luke, the author of this Gospel, begins relating this story with a
description that this was just a normal day on the ministry calendar
of Jesus. It wasn't a Sabbath or a large public gathering; most likely it
was a private home with a group of curious Pharisees and teachers. It
was just "one of those days."

But even on "one of those days," Jesus had extraordinary power to
heal. In Luke 5:17-26, Jesus heals a paralytic through the persistent
and compassionate care of his friends. They believed that a full room
was no barrier to getting their companion in front of Jesus. Jesus was
fueled with the inexhaustible resource of God. It is this power to heal
that compelled Jesus to declare the health of the soul before the healing of the body. "Man, your sins are forgiven you" (5:20). A broken
body was the second focus of our Lord. The power to heal was first
applied to the most profound need.

My guess is that the Pharisees and teachers viewed themselves as
whole and complete, but Jesus' declaration was intended to highlight
the paralysis that existed in their hearts and souls. Jesus had diag-
nosed their problem long before the roof started to come down. He
knew that self-righteousness had paralyzed the hearts and minds of

the religious zealots. He had "the power of the Lord" to heal. But only for those who understood their need.

I've had "one of those days" . . . a non-spectacular twenty-four-hour period where I wonder if God has shifted His attention to more important matters—quite frequently. In that moment, on those terms, Luke 5 reminds me that even ordinary days are reserved for the extraordinary working of God to heal, to mend, to inspire, to restore, to propel, to convict, to mobilize, to expose the paralysis of my own soul.

Yes, on one of those days . . .

LIGHT OF
THE WORLD

You are the light of the world. A city set on a hill cannot be hidden. Nor do people light
a lamp and put it under a basket, but on a stand, and it gives light to all in the house.
In the same way, let your light shine before others, so that they may see your good
works and give glory to your Father who is in heaven.

(MATTHEW 5:14-16)

WHILE I HAD SWEATY palms, a knot in my stomach, a blockade
forming in my throat, the Master of Ceremonies dutifully stepped to
the microphone and read my bio in an attempt to construct a platform of credibility before I moved to the podium.

This was true at the start of the ministry of Jesus. Matthew 4:15, 16
draws from the well of the prophet Isaiah and proclaims to all mankind, "The people dwelling in darkness have seen a great light, and for
those dwelling in the region and shadow of death, on them a light has
dawned."

That was it . . . the next words of Matthew 4 declare, "From that
time Jesus began to preach, saying, 'Repent, for the kingdom of heaven
is at hand'" (4:17).

Light described what the world will never extinguish.

Light was the résumé used to define the credibility of the Son of
God. The venue for the explosion of this light was "the region and
shadow of death." Yes, light for those of us who have an address envel-
oped in suffocating darkness.

Then Jesus changes roles and introduces us. And as He does so in
the Matthew 5 passage above, He transfers to us the privilege of being
the ambassadors of the credential that defines Him.

We become the penetrating presence of the living light. We obliterate what evil invents. We shine . . . and the city has no explanation except for the power of God.

His bio becomes ours. Yes, the Light introduces us. When we live as He plans for us to live, there is nothing—no power of hell or scheme of man—that can overcome what God ignites.

"On them a light has dawned."

Indeed, a bio for all eternity.

The Gate and the Golden Rule

Enter by the narrow gate. For the gate is wide and the way is easy that leads to destruction, and those who enter by it are many. For the gate is narrow and the way is hard that leads to life, and those who find it are few.

(Matthew 7:13, 14)

HE HAD THE CROWD leaning in on every word. His insights had captivated their hearts, minds, and souls. His message was uncluttered with political baggage, and His lifestyle defied anything they had witnessed before. This guy was amazing.

So about the time that He landed on "the Golden Rule" in His most famous of all sermons, the crowd was agreeing, smiling, and ready to join the bandwagon of this new religious teacher. "So whatever you wish that others would do to you, do also to them" (Matthew 7:12), Yes, words to live by.

But you'll notice that Jesus didn't close in prayer at that point. He didn't dust off His best, most inclusive, camera-ready smile and wave a politician's wave. No, Jesus hit the crowd with one of His most difficult realities before the oxygen of the Golden Rule had fully expanded their chests.

While heads were still nodding in agreement, Jesus reeled off a string of non-tolerant, non-inclusive, non-marketing-friendly words that had to feel like an ice-cold bucket of water right after a warm and comforting bath: narrow, destruction, hard, few.

Jesus resisted the growing political momentum to sway Him off course from the reason for His existence. There was no tidal wave of popular opinion strong enough to pull Him off His anchor. Jesus' words were a hot dagger through an ice-cold religion.

In the end, Jesus knew that a more "marketing friendly" gospel was not good news at all. The power of sacrificial action (the Golden Rule) came when it was birthed out of the womb of heartfelt repentance. It's the narrow gate that leads to life, a turnstile with a ticket taker.

Jesus' offer of hope included authentic and demanding realities. But isn't that what makes it good news? Isn't that what compelled Him to come? Isn't He the only one who understands what's required at the turnstile?

Perhaps these were some of His most compassionate words, for they underscore the cost of authentic hope. Yes indeed, this is the Golden Rule.

MADE NEW

*I will give you a new heart, and a new spirit I will put within you. And I will remove
the heart of stone from your flesh and give you a heart of flesh.*

(EZEKIEL 36:26)

DO YOU BUY USED stuff? Websites like Craigslist.com and many
others have galvanized the used marketplace in a way that classified
ads never could.

Some time ago, I began looking for a used lawn mower. While I
would have liked to spring for a shiny new model from Home Depot,
the size of my yard hardly justified the expense. So I watched for an
adequate piece of used equipment. Hoping all the while that the oil-
leaking, bailing-wire model I was presently using would hang together
until the proverbial handoff of the baton. It owed me nothing, years
of faithful service had proven that, but I was not afraid to keep pulling
the cord to request one more round.

While "used" may be great stewardship, it's an unfortunate miscon-
ception in our spiritual life. When the message of Christ is communicated adequately, it invites us to the showroom, not a garage sale.

Therefore, if anyone is in Christ, he is a new creation.
The old has passed away; behold, the new has come.

(2 CORINTHIANS 5:17)

No refurbished parts. No stains, dents, or dings from past use or
abuse ... but a new heart, a new life, a hope-filled start. Born new ...
again.

We trade our oil-leaking engines for shiny new lives. This is the
good news.

Any shame is not just covered over; it's replaced with a hope and a future.

From Goodwill to Nordstrom. From Craigslist.com to the Detroit Auto Show.

I've seen the shame and pain in the face of a 17 year old and I've offered her more than a makeover. I've offered Jesus.

Religion is like putting a fresh coat of paint on a 1991 Oldsmobile; following Christ means we roll off the assembly line brand new.

This is why we can never stop talking about Jesus. This is why we have to go everywhere. This is why we go to tough places with rough people. It's why we're not fooled by a façade of power and success. For as certainly as there are oil-leaking engines in our urban corridors, they are evident in corporate boardrooms and church pews as well.

Nothing, absolutely nothing makes us new except the love and blood of Jesus. He paid for the exchange and didn't shop at Craigslist.

A soul transformed. New. What hope. What a promise.

Soli Deo gloria.

WOW ME, LORD!

And they were astonished beyond measure, saying,
"He has done all things well."

(MARK 7:37)

WHAT ASTONISHES YOU? What arrests your mind with amaze-ment? Are there things in your life that stop you in your tracks with astonishment?

Maybe you're like me. Perhaps you prefer the predictable patterns of life. Clear, definable boundaries, patterns with edges, effects that result from known causes.

But I'm not sure that's the way God works. A dozen times in the Gospel of Mark alone, the reaction of the people to the life of Christ is described in the terminology of awe, the scriptural equivalent of "Wow!"

And immediately all the crowd, when they saw him, were greatly amazed
and ran up to him and greeted him.

(MARK 9:15)

And he got into the boat with them, and the wind ceased.
And they were utterly astounded.

(MARK 6:51)

Maybe the problem is that I'm wowed by the wrong things. Maybe I'm captivated by the gift—an accomplished musician, a talented athlete, a brilliant invention, an act of love—instead of the giver.

Maybe God's next act of "wow" is available, but unrequested. Do I ask for God to astonish, to amaze, to astound? Am I afraid, too proud, or too weak?

> And Jesus said to him, "If you can! All things are possible for one who believes." Immediately the father of the child cried out and said, "I believe; help my unbelief!"
>
> (MARK 9:23, 24)

That's it—the admission of an honest man. "I believe; help my unbelief!" Wow me, God! Please! Show up in unscripted times. Work in unplanned ways. Walk on uncharted seas. Claim undeeded land. Heal. Fix. Send.

O Lord, the invitation is out there. My heart is ready. My need is great. My blinders are off. The distractions are gone.

Astound, amaze, and astonish. Please.

COME AND
LISTEN

Jesus entered a village. And a woman named Martha welcomed him into her house.
And she had a sister called Mary, who sat at the Lord's feet and listened to his teaching.
But Martha was distracted with much serving.

(LUKE 10:38-40)

NOBLE INTENTIONS PRODUCED A cluttered soul, and with it a squandered opportunity to harvest the moments of solitude with Jesus.

And when noble intentions take a back seat to a hungry heart, our minds absorb the very words of God. We listen. We cease doing so that we have room to contain the richness of His message.

God, the great I Am, not only breathes life into our nostrils, He chooses to speak words of life into our soul. The glorious treasure of His truth is generously and clearly dispersed to those who discard lesser things, even to the point of delegating noble activities to lower places because those activities may compromise the profound moments at the feet of the Messiah.

Outstanding causes become distractions if they detour us from the feet of Jesus. Acts of mercy and justice return empty handed if they are not launched from the embrace of Christ. Our passion to serve emerges when we have visited the humility that comes from sitting in submission at the feet of the King.

"You have the words of eternal life" (John 6:68). But sometimes we are too busy for words. We are doing and serving, talking and training, helping and reaching, all the while missing the point.

I invite you to take a break from doing. Come and recharge your soul by listening to Jesus' teaching.

From the vantage point of His feet, we see the world in a completely different way. We hear His words with amazing clarity.

First things first: at the feet of Jesus.

A LOST SHEEP

*What man of you, having a hundred sheep, if he has lost one of them, does not leave
the ninety-nine in the open country, and go after the one that is lost, until he finds it?
And when he has found it, he lays it on his shoulders, rejoicing.*

(LUKE 15:4, 5)

NURSERY RHYMES HAVE BECOME a mainstay of our reading
resources for Malia, our two-year-old granddaughter. One day as she
listened intently to the occupational challenges that Bo Peep faced, I
listened intently to the approach that this fictional shepherd took to
retrieve her sheep.

> *Little Bo Peep has lost her sheep,*
> *And can't tell where to find them.*
> *Leave them alone, and they'll come home*
> *Wagging their tails behind them.*

"Leave them alone, and they'll come home. . . ." Really? Lost sheep,
wandering, separated and distant will eventually drift back home? Not
only will they come prancing home, but their tails will be wagging
in delight. I'm not sure that this concept has been appropriately and
accurately vetted. Has an audit been performed on the veracity of this
claim?

Jesus might take issue with this strategy. He might argue that lost
sheep will never find their way home, that separated and distant they
become vulnerable. Unlike Bo Peep, Jesus drops everything to pursue.
He knows that lost sheep become an easy target . . . and that a pursuing, focused, and passionate shepherd is the only rescuer.

Leave them alone versus pursue at all cost.

They'll come home versus go after the one that is lost.

Wagging their tails versus shoulders to rest upon and an exuberant shepherd.

Our way versus the gospel.

The good news of Jesus Christ is radical.

Sheep wander.

Sheep don't stroll back home after a good day on the range.

Good shepherds don't just hang around and wait.

Lost sheep don't wag their tails.

Jesus, our shepherd, pursued us. He loves us. He leaves the rescued to find the lost.

He sets a standard that Bo Peep could learn from, and in doing so, He demonstrates that God's plan is no nursery rhyme. It's dirty, and dangerous, and costly, and effective.

Lost sheep . . . every last one of them . . . need a shepherd: a real shepherd; a courageous and committed shepherd.

AGAIN AND IMMEDIATELY

Again he went away and prayed, saying the same words. And again he came and found them sleeping, for their eyes were very heavy, and they did not know what to answer him. And he came the third time and said to them, "Are you still sleeping and taking your rest? It is enough; the hour has come. The Son of Man is betrayed into the hands of sinners. Rise, let us be going; see, my betrayer is at hand." And immediately, while he was still speaking, Judas came, one of the twelve, and with him a crowd with swords and clubs, from the chief priests and the scribes and the elders.

(MARK 14:39-43)

AGAIN AND *IMMEDIATELY*: TWO words that show a Savior in pain. Jesus made a request of three of His disciples—Peter, James and John—His closest allies, His trusted friends, His inner circle, and all they could deliver was disappointment. Sleep was more urgent than loyalty. And so, once again, as Jesus dialoged with the Father in ultimate earnestness, His earthly comrades drifted off. His pain found no partner, His turmoil no companion.

As if this wasn't enough, immediately Jesus is confronted with the betrayal of His treasurer: the man who knew the inner workings of the ministry; the man in whom great trust had been placed; the man whose feet Jesus had just washed with His own hands. Unlike the other disciples, this man was not just passively rebelling; he was an active traitor masquerading as a kissing confidant.

Again and immediately. Alone and abandoned. Ignored and betrayed.

Is there any point of disappointment in our lives that Jesus hasn't experienced more acutely? No wound from a friend, no pain of deceit, no willful act of denial and neglect that Jesus hasn't experienced more profoundly.

Again and immediately. Jesus knows our pain. Not indirectly. Not from a safe distance, but in the garden at the point of our greatest need and exposure. Some sleeping, some stealing His trust.

Our Savior has plumbed the depth of our greatest pain . . . and has offered us hope, and healing through the cross. He is more than empathetic; He is our companion in the desert, our guide through the desperation.

Giving Out of Poverty

They all contributed out of their abundance, but she out of her poverty has put in everything she had, all she had to live on.

(Mark 12:44)

AS JESUS PEERS ACROSS the temple, He looks deeply into the souls of the congregants. He wasn't auditing their actions; instead, He was investigating their hearts and assessing their motivation.

His description and commendation of the widow rings into the darkest recesses of my own patterns of living and giving. When Jesus highlights and applauds the strategy of giving "out of her poverty," I am convicted to the core. The implication and application of this truth is vital in my understanding of the love of Christ as it transparently reveals the depth of my trust in His care for me.

I've learned to risk . . . only from a place of safety.

To love . . . only from a place of security.

To defend . . . only from a place of certainty.

To explore . . . only from a place of predictability.

To dream . . . only from a place of realism.

To give . . . only from a place of plenty.

This is not the plan of Jesus. It is not His approach to living with the abandon of a soul set free. Jesus trumpets the concept of generous living from a place of desperation and brokenness.

We love . . . because He first loved us.

We give . . . because He emptied the treasury of heaven for us.

We risk . . . because our safety is found in Christ alone.

We forgive . . . because He forgave.

We defend the defenseless . . . because it was for them that He wielded His sword.

We abandon bias and prejudice . . . because His assessment of the soul is beyond our ability.

We reconcile . . . because He alone is judge.

We give "out of our poverty" . . . because it is there that we can plumb the depth of our worth in Him.

It is no sacrifice to give from a full account. And Jesus, our model and master, knows the pain of our sacrifice, the depth of the well from which our gifts are given. Jesus knows.

From across the temple He looks intently . . . and as He does, He sees well beyond my action and clearly into my motivation and sacrifice.

I give and live from a place of confidence in Jesus, not the safety of self-reliance.

It is out of our poverty that we tap into the limitless love of Jesus.

THE BEAUTY OF
TRANSFORMATION

Now there is in Jerusalem by the Sheep Gate a pool, in Aramaic called Bethesda,
which has five roofed colonnades. In these lay a multitude of invalids—blind, lame,
and paralyzed. One man was there who had been an invalid for thirty-eight years.

(JOHN 5:2-5)

FOR THIRTY-EIGHT YEARS THIS man was an invalid. Always late to the healing whirlpool. Never the object of the healing. No friend or advocate . . . until Jesus. Then, history and heartache are transcended with a direct command: "Get up, take up your bed, and walk" (5:8).

And that's exactly what he did. No rehab or physical therapy necessary. Bone strength and muscle tone exploded into mobility. At the sound of the Master's voice, cells, tissue, blood vessels, tendons, joints, and nerves saluted in ready response. Once broken, once lame, once confined to life on the edge of hope, now reconstructed. Instantly.

Obediently, the man walked into a religious speed trap. The Jews were ready, at least to catch the offenders. But they were unprepared for the shattering effect of Jesus' love, compassion, and mercy. It was uncontainable, and seemingly irreverent. And so, the Sabbath soldiers attacked. And what a moment to attack: at the euphoric moment of restoration, in the narthex of the sanctuary of celebration. When all of the joy and glee expressed on the inside can finally be appropriately expressed on the outside, the delight gets handcuffed.

When legalism strangles grace, we stop celebrating the miracles of God. We're suspicious when He works, and we dissect every act of mercy. We can't believe His extravagant love, so we tax it. We ask the wrong questions. We profane the beauty of transformation with doubt or jealousy.

Legalism highlights the infraction, while grace restores the soul.

At long last, after thirty-eight years, the man at Bethesda could carry his own mat, and as he did he exposed the crippled souls of the religious zealots.

Yes indeed, the Messiah is in the house; He's changing everything . . . and exposing the fraud, even today.

IN CLOSE PROXIMITY

When the large crowd of the Jews learned that Jesus was there, they came, not only on account of him but also to see Lazarus, whom he had raised from the dead. So the chief priests made plans to put Lazarus to death as well, because on account of him many of the Jews were going away and believing in Jesus.

(JOHN 12:9-11)

SHOTS RANG OUT ON East 37th Street in Denver as a 2004 Dodge Stratus raced through an urban community. The act of violence was gang related, and while the target was known, not all of the bullets found their mark. In fact, two of them struck Yazmine Sandate, and her sister, Karina Padilla. While both girls will recover physically, this drive-by shooting highlights the fact that many times in our communities people are "proximity victims." Because they were close to the scene of the crime, the line of innocence was crossed. They were involved because they were there.

As the start of the Passion Week began in the life of Jesus, we read the above account from John 12:9-11. These verses are tucked between Mary anointing Jesus' feet and the Triumphal Entry. They describe the growing hatred of the chief priests toward Jesus as He grows in popularity. But in the spray of hatred and evil planning, Lazarus gets caught in the crossfire. Yes Lazarus. Once dead now alive. He's not a troublemaker; he's just a Jesus follower. He lives his life in close proximity to the Lord. He should, Jesus was his life giver . . . literally. He's an exhibit of the power of this Jewish carpenter, so because he's in the neighborhood, because he walks the sidewalks of Jesus' neighborhood, because his life reflects the address of the Messiah, he becomes a target; a potential drive-by victim in Messianic proportion.

Our proximity to Jesus may just make us a target. The blasts from the gun of the enemy may often strike those closest to the Savior. Like Lazarus, the light of our testimony may be enough to attract the fire of evil.

But don't lose heart . . . Jesus understands and cares for us. In John 16:33 Jesus declares: "I have said these things to you, that in me you may have peace. In the world you will have tribulation. But take heart; I have overcome the world."

Remember, no fear. Jesus has overcome the world. But remember as well, the closer you come to the Lord, the more the hatred focused on Him may find its way to you.

May our proximity to Jesus implicate us.

A CALL TO SURRENDER

Simon Peter, having a sword, drew it and struck the high priest's servant and cut off his right ear.

(JOHN 18:10)

IT WAS A NIGHTTIME walk across the Kidron Valley into a garden, a familiar place for Jesus and His disciples. But the moist evening air was split by a band of soldiers with torches, weapons, and lanterns.

Jesus knew their intent and the significance of the moment. So He stepped forward. He embraced His call, even in the shadows of false accusation and betrayal.

In the confusion and chaos, Peter reacted. Having a sword, he drew it and used it. And when he used it, he exposed the natural tendency of all of us.

When His plans aren't my plans . . . I draw *my* sword.

When the circumstances exceed my explanation . . . I draw *my* sword.

When I'm confronted with unexpected disappointment . . . I draw *my* sword.

When a friend crosses the line . . . I draw *my* sword.

When I forget the purposes of God . . . I draw *my* sword.

When I want to do something, anything . . . I draw *my* sword.

When I don't take time to pray, or even think . . . I draw *my* sword.

When a familiar place becomes a hostile place . . . I draw *my* sword.

When God simply doesn't seem to come through . . . I draw *my* sword.

When the angels, legions of them, stand on the sideline . . . I draw *my* sword.

When rumors swirl and people talk . . . I draw *my* sword.

When the morning mail is disappointing . . . I draw *my* sword.

When I think God is too silent . . . I draw *my* sword.

When the morning commute is, the morning commute . . . I draw *my* sword.

When I get really, really painful or difficult news . . . I draw *my* sword.

When I can't explain why . . . I draw *my* sword.

When my alarm clock becomes my troubled heart . . . I draw *my* sword.

When I think it's my job to fix instead of obey . . . I draw *my* sword.

When I follow Peter instead of Jesus . . . I draw *my* sword.

I stop trusting.

I stop listening.

I stop believing.

I stop waiting.

I quit remembering.

I draw *my* sword.

Jesus could have, but didn't.

Jesus said, "No more of this!" (Luke 22:51).

A call to surrender to the purposes of God all the way to the cross.

I draw *my* sword no more.

Will you surrender?

THE ONLY WAY

Jesus said to [Thomas], "I am the way, and the truth, and the life.
No one comes to the Father except through me."

(JOHN 14:6)

ONE TUESDAY NIGHT I fulfilled a baseball "to do" on my list of parks to visit . . . Yankee Stadium. What a blast. As we crossed the 161st Street bridge and approached the stadium, I noticed a small, open, grass-covered area adjacent to the ballpark. In the modest green space was a team of very small, identically dressed boys. They tossed a ball back and forth, following the instruction of an adult who seemed to be doing his best to coach the team.

Twenty minutes later, I was sitting in a seat on the opposite side of the stucco exterior of Yankee Stadium, not more than a hundred yards from where we had witnessed baseball practice in action. What a difference one hundred yards makes.

On one side of the stadium wall, boys dream and aspire; on the other, they make good on the promises they make. On one side, they play in anonymity; on the other, they wear pinstriped uniforms with their last name stitched on the back. On one side, they pay to play; on the other, the collective fortunes of the team amount to over $194 million in a year. On one side, the encroaching darkness pronounces the activities complete; on the other, cascading electricity-produced light ushers in hours of entertainment. On one side, boys dream in the shadows of Yankee Stadium; on the other, gifted athletes perform at the peak of their personal performance.

One hundred yards. Just one hundred yards ... and yet a world away. Proximity is no license for entry, no ticket to the field of play. For Alex, Derek, Jason, Mike, and Johnny, there were no shortcuts to this venue.

In the fourteenth chapter of the book of John, Thomas, the disciple, asked Jesus to describe "the way."

The only way to move the impossible distance to God is with Jesus. On the one side, dreams of significance, hope, life; on the other, we are children of the living God.

One hundred yards ... no shortcuts. Jesus alone.

No longer in the shadows, but in the wonderful, eternal light.

HE'S PREPARED

Let not your hearts be troubled. Believe in God; believe also in me. In my Father's house are many rooms. If it were not so, would I have told you that I go to prepare a place for you? And if I go and prepare a place for you, I will come again and will take you to myself, that where I am you may be also.

(JOHN 14:1-3)

I KNEW THAT MAKING my connecting flight was going to be a long shot, but my heart was still engaged in hope. I raced through the jetway as quickly as possible to get a glimpse at the departures board. A flight to Denver wasn't even on the board . . . not mine, and nobody else's. I was stuck at Dulles Airport in Washington, D.C. and there was nothing I could do about it.

A trip to a kiosk confirmed that I had been rebooked on a 6 a.m. flight, and so the "bad news" phone calls began. By this time it was late, very late, and the concept of traveling to a local hotel for a very few hours of sleep seemed like an unjustifiable expense. So I invoked my best survival skills and started planning for an overnight on a Dulles Airport bench.

I was in the main terminal, and it was now about 11:30 p.m. It felt like a ghost town. The open spaces were vacant and still. The prerecorded PA announcements bounced off the curved ceilings and around the expansive atrium like a cue ball against the rails of a pool table.

I had made the best use of an overcoat and four days of laundry to establish a padded sleeping area . . . I was quite a sight. By this time it was midnight, and my desire for rest was on a collision course with an unexpected invasion. It was subtle at first, but then in waves, airport maintenance personnel assaulted the tasks in front of them. One drove an impressive sweeper/polisher, another walked around with a putty knife looking for inappropriately discarded gum and scraped what couldn't be swept and shouldn't be polished. Another team of three worked to replace fluorescent light bulbs above ticket counters. Others vacuumed, some emptied, a few arranged—all with focus, purpose and effectiveness.

By 3:45 a.m., the automatic doors started to slide open in an act of obedience to the arriving passengers. By 4 a.m., the place was alive and ready. Dulles International Airport was once again ready for planned and unplanned activity.

Every night and every day, Jesus is getting ready for you, for those who embrace His grace. While I do my best to make my way through another day in exile, the Savior doesn't sleep.

"I will come again and will take you to myself." He's prepared.

He loves us that much.

FULL JOY

These things I have spoken to you, that my joy may be in you,
and that your joy may be full.

(JOHN 15:11)

OVER TWENTY-FIVE YEARS AGO as I knelt next to a bathtub in our home in Fort Wayne, I had a singular purpose in mind . . . scrub the boys and remove the unwanted remnants of a day of play. Wash cloth, soap, and elbow grease provided the necessary tools to perform the crisply bordered activities that were associated with bath time.

An unwritten but fully understood parameter around this time was that a successful bath time was only possible if the water remained confined. Splashing and spraying were strictly forbidden.

On a Tuesday night, I was once again in the familiar kneeling position next to a tub—this time in Aurora, Colorado; this time it was two young girls in the tub . . . Malia and Davey, my granddaughters.

Mary tended to the functional aspects of the bathing while I, incrementally, enthusiastically, and with full participation, broke each of the water-confinement rules I had established over twenty-five years before. I methodically refilled squirting toys and handed them to Malia so that she could randomly shoot whatever she wished . . . including me. She giggled . . . and I laughed. Her eyes lit up . . . even as she watched mine do the same.

The girls splashed, sprayed, poured sometimes inside the walled confines and yes, sometimes not. And not only did I not care, I encouraged, openly fanning the flame of celebration and joy.

When we live life . . . really live life . . . water splashes. Sometimes it stays obediently inside the parameters we've defined, but sometimes it escapes. Sometimes it gets stuff wet; sometimes it goes where we hadn't really planned for it to go.

And as joy splashes outside its boundaries ... something wonderful happens ...

It may have taken decades, but I've finally learned what bath time is all about. Andrew and Erik, I'm sorry I missed this point.

Splash more.

Spontaneous, unbounded, unscripted, beautiful life.

Life that gets dry things wet; life that requires a little cleanup at the end; life that reflects sacrifice, risk, courage, and celebration. But Jesus promises that our joy will be full.

Yes, splash more. Life to the full. Buckets and squirt toys included.

A SPIRITUAL REBOOT

For God so loved the world, that he gave his only Son, that whoever believes in him should not perish but have eternal life. For God did not send his Son into the world to condemn the world, but in order that the world might be saved through him.

(JOHN 3:16, 17)

THE WEIGHT OF POLITICAL pressure had begun to intensify around the ministry and messages of Jesus. He was making the religious power brokers very nervous. The focus of the public eye had shifted, and the authentic love of the teacher from Nazareth was turning heads as quickly as it was changing lives.

Skeptics and critics protested and schemed, but their complaints were a cover-up for their selfishness and pride. The religious natives were growing restless as control oozed out of their greedy hands. Fear and intimidation was being replaced with hope and love.

So it was no wonder that Nicodemus used night to cloak his inquisitive heart, and Jesus responded, not with words of compromise, but with a powerful and provocative metaphor: "Unless you are born again, you cannot see the Kingdom of God" (John 3:3, NLT). To which Nicodemus basically replied, "What do you mean?" (3:4)

This genuine response illustrates just how mind-boggling Jesus' remedy for the human condition was. It was as though He said, "You have to understand Nicodemus, this is not an incremental step along the pharisaical journey. This is about a new start, about creation and not cosmetics. This is a reset, reboot, rebirth kind of change."

Jesus embraced the call of the seeker with the friendliest message possible: transformation truth. Moments later, Jesus ushered this wondering heart to his seat inside the concert hall of grace.

Jesus came not to condemn, but to save. How non-pharisaical. In fact, this called into question the very heart of the job description for a Pharisee. They were judge and jury. They were the hired "religion cops," the sheriffs of spirituality. And Jesus rebuffed the badge with a birthday.

The plight of the human condition demands unvarnished answers. Transformation is provocative. Old men climbing back into their mother's womb probably wouldn't be defined as "seeker friendly," but pouring truth into hollow religious constructs is likely to burst old wineskins.

> *Therefore, if anyone is in Christ, he is a new creation.*
>
> (2 CORINTHIANS 5:17)

What could offer more hope to the atrophied heart of a sinner than a second shot at being created?

We need light, not polish, over the message of Jesus. "Unless you are born again" . . . indeed!

175

HE MUST
INCREASE

Everyone is going to him instead of coming to us.

(JOHN 3:26, NLT)

MARKET SHARE. IT'S ALL about market share. John's disciples were studiously monitoring trends in ministry trajectory. The Baptizer was at his peak. He was baptizing, with customers still in the queue. But his astute disciples noticed a disturbing trend: "Everyone is going to him [Jesus] instead of coming to us." In other words: "We're in trouble!"

The flip charts were up; the markers were drawn with caps off. Let's analyze this situation. "What is He offering that we aren't?" "How are His recruiting efforts succeeding and ours are hemorrhaging?" "What's this guy's value proposition?"

John the Baptist was a bulldog. His disciples had spent enough time with him to know that. He was undaunted in his mission and unfazed by resistance. He wore the uniform of sacrifice and ate at the training table of personal discipline. He had taken on all comers, and now it appeared to his followers that Jesus was locked in his sights. "Bring it on!" they seemed to taunt.

"I am not the Messiah. I am only here to prepare the way for him" (John 3:28, NLT).

Are you kidding! The stage hand and not the star?

This wasn't a floundering ministry star passing the baton to the next generation. This wasn't an exercise in succession planning. This was a booster engine propelling a rocket ship. This was a prophet giving way to the Messiah.

At the pinnacle of his personal success, John deferred to the plan of God.

This was John, submitting his agenda to The Agenda: "He must increase, but I must decrease" (John 3:30).

There was no white flag of surrender. This was a willful act of worship. "It was never about me. Never!"

John the Baptist did what every marketing and PR firm in the world couldn't . . . he delivered a personal mission statement for every follower of Jesus. Every one of us.

Forever and always . . . He must be the bull's-eye on the target, the objective of the plan, the return on every investment.

Whatever our personal agenda, organizational mission, corporate identity, or market niche regardless of how noble, it's secondary. "He must increase." If John, then certainly me.

"Everyone is going to him instead of coming to us." May it be so.

COMMUNITY

The Word became flesh and dwelt among us, and we have seen his glory,
glory as of the only Son from the Father, full of grace and truth.

(JOHN 1:14)

AN OLD MACHINE SHOP on the urban streets of Winnipeg, Manitoba, Canada has been an indoor skate park for eighteen years. And on Thursday night when I walked in the front door of The Edge, I could sense something different, something unique, something redemptive.

It was a noisy place. Certainly well used. The largest part of the structure was unobstructed, but filled with unique ramps, protruding rails, and plywood jumps. Every inch of the place was in play, accessible. And as I stood, young men on boards screamed past me, jumping, flipping their boards, twisting, falling . . . in full speed.

A group of us went upstairs to a small meeting area that had a smaller kitchen attached. We listened to Cliff, the director of The Edge. He talked about the history, the mission, and the focus. He talked about the hundreds of kids who find warmth and recreation during the unforgiving and relentless winter months in Winnipeg. He then introduced us to a young man, a twelve year old. Nervously he spouted his first name . . . it was something like Meesh.

He was uncomfortable until he began talking about what The Edge means to him. Like a moth to the light on your front step, Meesh kept gravitating to a single word to describe The Edge.

Community.

"It's my family. It's where I come to skate, to be with friends, to eat, to read the Bible, and to learn about God. It's my community." Over and over. With pride. With confidence. Because he was talking about something that he loved.

At the corner of Lily and Pacific, there is an old unassuming building. But inside, something transformational happens. Young men learn what it's like to play hard together. What it's like to cheer for each other. What it's like to eat a meal together. And what can happen when you understand that you and God can walk through life together.

It's at The Edge that the incarnation of Jesus happens. It's there that God puts on skin. It's there that isolation and loneliness give way to community. It's there that peer pressure is redirected, that expectations are elevated, that hope is birthed . . . that Jesus lives among us.

I met a young man who told us that he has a family . . . at The Edge.

This is where good news becomes the Good News.

I was inspired and moved, because I met Meesh. Because Meesh met Jesus at The Edge.

Yes, the Word dwelling among, and shining the glory . . . full of grace and truth . . . and skateboards and volunteers and teenagers and hope and forgiveness and love and promise and family . . . and community.

Where are you making Christ known? Where are you living the incarnation?

179

HE NEVER
LETS GO

My sheep hear my voice, and I know them, and they follow me. I give them eternal life, and they will never perish, and no one will snatch them out of my hand. My Father, who has given them to me, is greater than all, and no one is able to snatch them out of the Father's hand. I and the Father are one.

(JOHN 10:27-30)

FROM THE LIPS OF the perfect Son of God, Jesus warrants the safety of our soul on the credibility of His Father. His grip is more than secure. His grasp is more than tight.

Jesus knew. He was well aware that the uncertainty of our situations would have to collide with a force of devastating strength. He knew that self-confidence, affluence, pride, self-pity, or power would provide the green grass that attracts wandering sheep. He knew that the enemy—crafty, deceptive, evil, polluted, hateful and attractive— would do everything and anything to draw us.

That is why Jesus uses metaphor and not parable. He wanted to make sure that there was absolutely no missing His guarantee. "No one," and again, "no one" will snatch them out of the Father's hand. And Jesus declares that His Father "is greater than all."

Sheep like us prone to wander, now riveted to the palm of Almighty.

I'm certain that Jesus knew that there would be times in all of our lives when we would wonder, when we would doubt, when events and pain and catastrophe would wedge a crowbar against our resolve, which is exactly why He anchored our confidence in "My Father." The I Am. The Creator.

The limitless grip of God holds us tight. He will never let us go. He will never relinquish control.

The voice of the Shepherd is reassuring. He makes promises and keeps them.

"My Father . . . is greater than all, and no one is able to snatch them out of the Father's hand."

Nothing, no one, never.

LORD, IT'S YOU

After this many of his disciples turned back and no longer walked with him. So Jesus said to the Twelve, "Do you want to go away as well?" Simon Peter answered him, "Lord, to whom shall we go? You have the words of eternal life, and we have believed, and have come to know, that you are the Holy One of God."

(JOHN 6:66-69)

I HADN'T PLANNED ON needing directions, but that was the way the evening had gone. I was on my bike in an unfamiliar park in Denver. I had parked my van and ridden off just about an hour before, but an unexpected cloud burst and diminishing light had disrupted my orientation. It was with a growing sense of helplessness that I approached a fisherman loading his gear into his truck. I needed directions. The man seemed to be able to decipher my cryptic description of the parking lot I was looking for, and much to my delight pointed in a southerly direction and said, "It's just over there."

With prompt obedience, I peddled off in the direction he had pointed. But he was wrong. Either his understanding of what I was looking for or his knowledge of the park itself had made his directions worse than useless. I peddled harder and harder, but I was going the wrong direction. No amount of energy or drive was going to solve that problem.

In the sixth chapter of the book of John, Jesus is giving some unpopular direction to His followers. His solution to their lostness involved personal sacrifice and absolute compliance. And it clearly made some in the audience very uncomfortable. In fact, some individuals left. The tough teaching made them opt out. So Jesus, in classic style, asks a question to the Twelve, "Do you want to go away as well?" Peter's pragmatic answer rings through time with crisp clarity.

Who else could we go and hang out with who has the answers to life like You do? You're the guy, Jesus. Your words breathe life into dead souls. We may not like the directions, Lord, but You're going to tell it straight. You're going to help us find the way.

Difficult truth beats palatable lies every time. Momentary optimism quickly gives way to lostness. We need real answers. Real solutions. Real direction.

So here's my prayer: Lord, it's You, the compass of my soul. No shortcuts . . . but real hope. Solutions. It's You . . . and You alone. Peter was right. May we be as bold and brave as he was. Thanks for showing us the way. Thanks for giving us answers that work. Amen.

Where else? Who else? Nowhere and no one but Jesus.

SAY YES
TO NO

[Jesus] called to him the crowd with his disciples and said to them,
"If anyone would come after me, let him deny himself and take up his cross
and follow me. For whoever would save his life will lose it,
but whoever loses his life for my sake and the gospel's will save it."

(MARK 8:34, 35)

IN AN ACT OF domestic solidarity one day, I joined Mary in putting clean sheets on a couple of the extra beds that we have in our house. I also noticed that Mary had homemade lasagna in the refrigerator that was just waiting for the appropriate guests to arrive. Yes, their arrival would provide multiple opportunities for us to welcome and entertain guests in our home. Mary wanted to be ready.

This activity cascaded a light of revelation on the season of Lent. In the Christian tradition, Lent represents the forty days prior to Easter. They are intended to be days of preparation, reflection, worship, and self-denial.

Self-denial fascinates me.

We live in a time and a culture that believes that we are entitled to "yes to yes" and "no to no." Saying "yes to no" is not only countercultural, it's often ridiculed as old-fashioned and perhaps even legalistic. Yet I believe that this very act of self-denial, this process of saying no to the things in our lives that are permissible, will ignite a bonfire of intimacy and worship that is not only important, it's vital. This kind of preparation cultivates a place of invitation and expectation . . . it does the laundry, the vacuuming, the dusting, the meal preparation, the candle lighting, and the ambiance setting before the guests ever arrive. Before the Guest arrives.

Saying "yes to no" makes room. It vacates our soul of the clutter that occupies needed space. It invites the power of the Holy Spirit to invade. It demonstrates that transformation has, and is, occurring. It elevates. It humbles.

I want to be ready.

I want to say yes to no . . . for the sake of more . . . to make room.

My checkbook. My meals. My calendar. My watch. My BlackBerry. My remote control. My agenda. My comfort. My attention. My entertainment.

Yes to no . . . so that I can say yes to Jesus . . . perhaps as never before.

THE WONDROUS CROSS

What then shall we say to these things? If God is for us, who can be against us? He who did not spare his own Son but gave him up for us all, how will he not also with him graciously give us all things? Who shall bring any charge against God's elect? It is God who justifies. Who is to condemn? Christ Jesus is the one who died—more than that, who was raised—who is at the right hand of God, who indeed is interceding for us.

(ROMANS 8:31-34)

*When I survey the wondrous cross
On which the Prince of Glory died;
My richest gain I count but loss,
And pour contempt on all my pride.*

IN A TIME OF corporate worship at the national office of Youth for Christ, we sang these powerful words penned by Isaac Watts in 1707. As I poured over the words that my lips produced, my soul raced to a question: When did the cross become wondrous? It seems preposterous to exclaim in melodious harmony that the cross—the symbol of shame, disgrace, pain, and retribution—could ever be described as wondrous.

As Jesus Himself anticipated the prospect of the cross, He cried out from His knees in the garden: "Abba, Father, all things are possible for you. Remove this cup from me. Yet not what I will, but what you will" (Mark 14:36). In this honest reflection of the horror of the cross, Jesus exposes the gravity of the event.

And so I ask again . . . was Isaac Watts correct? Has the cross become wondrous? What could ever transform an act of torture to a place of hope?

For the sake of justice . . . wondrous

For the demonstration of obedience to the Father . . . wondrous

For the modeling of humility . . . wondrous

For the selflessness . . . wondrous

For the bold rebuke of evil . . . wondrous

For the payment in full of my debt . . . wondrous

For the declaration that suffering is not defeat . . . wondrous

For the scandal of grace . . . wondrous

For the ultimate sacrifice . . . wondrous

For the pathway to resurrection . . . wondrous

For the gateway to God . . . wondrous

Yes, it is wondrous indeed.

So much to be thankful for, starting with the Wondrous Cross.

Sing to him; sing praises to him; tell of all his wondrous works!

(1 CHRONICLES 16:9)

HE IS WHO HE IS

God is light, and in him is no darkness at all.

(1 JOHN 1:5)

HAVE YOU EVER WONDERED if God is ready to change His public relations firm? It just seems to me that God is taking it in the chops these days in the press. There are so many stories of people who claim to be followers of Christ who fail and fall with a nationally and locally communicated thud.

The devastation to personal lives, to congregations, and to communities is played out in a public forum. Many times there is a direct connection to a Christian faith and often dogmatic stances.

So I ask you: Is God wringing His celestial hands wondering what to do next? Is He worried about His reputation?

In fact, there are items on His agenda that extend well beyond the sound bites of a cosmic press conference; things like justice, love, mercy, reconciliation, and confession. His plan pushes into the deep mire of personal failure. He doesn't debate about a cover-up or a carefully crafted press release. He's in favor of full disclose, not to shame but to expose. It is the only way to keep sin from festering. God never lurks in the shadows. He doesn't pass notes at night. He doesn't mask His voice. "God is light, and in him is no darkness at all." So the very splash across the front page is an amazing indicator that God is God. It's a demonstration that light always wins. That reputation is not the issue.

Our perfect, powerful God wades into the mess that mankind has made, the mess that Christ followers make . . . and He does so with dignity and grace. He does so with love and power. But He doesn't lower the standard. He chases and reveals for His name's sake. Yes, because He is God . . . even when people mock His name as a result.

So there will be no job posting on Hotjobs.com. The PR job has been spoken for with the forgiving and sacrificial stance of Jesus. This is about the redemption of tragically broken lives . . . not the reputation of a sinless God. He's not checking the poll numbers.

Justice, mercy, reconciliation . . . and hope through the disappointing headlines, the foolishness, the scandal, and the sacrilege. "I AM WHO I AM" (Exodus 3:14): That's His press release for the ages.

LIBERATED TO LOVE

For the love of Christ controls us, because we have concluded this: that one has died for all, therefore all have died; and he died for all, that those who live might no longer live for themselves but for him who for their sake died and was raised.

(2 CORINTHIANS 5:14, 15)

HAVE YOU EVER MET a control freak? You know, somebody who wants to be in charge of every situation in his life? I suppose we all have a bit of this tendency. It's a scripting strategy. Every situation anticipated, every action predefined, every behavior expected.

We couch this attitude inside the safe confines of statements like, "I just want to be in charge of my own destiny." Or, "God helps those who help themselves."

While I admit to this kind of predisposition, I would go on record as saying I believe it is an anti-God position.

The apostle Paul, a control-oriented kind of guy, pronounces with clarity and focus that the keys to the engine of every Christian should be the love of Christ. My actions and my desires should be powered by the understanding that love, a perfect, sacrificial, uncomplicated, unconditional love, is wrapped around me. No longer required, I am now liberated to obey. I am faithful, because I can't even imagine walking away from this love. I am selfless, because this love models in resounding tones the chorus of service and sacrifice.

Personal agendas disappear, acts of kindness move from a slogan to a reality. This is real love . . . this is real community . . . this is real Christian living.

Love liberates. It controls the head and heart so that hands willfully follow. It binds hearts to the heart of Christ. Moved, mounted, and maneuvered by what He wills and wants.

For the love of Christ . . . may it be so.

LIGHT WINS

The people who walked in darkness have seen a great light; those who dwelt in a land of deep darkness, on them has light shined.

(ISAIAH 9:2)

IT WAS A BLACKNESS that made even the possibility of vision out of the question. We were in the bowels of the earth exploring Mammoth Cave. Although it was many years ago, I still remember the feeling when the guide extinguished every light in the cave. The darkness was suffocating.

The universally accepted definition for darkness is "the absence of light." This clarity shines a profound spotlight on the many references in the Bible to darkness not only as an environmental condition ("Darkness was over the face of the deep" [Genesis 1:2]), but as the perfect picture of the non-believing soul ("For at one time you were darkness" [Ephesians 5:8]).

God's diagnosis of the human condition was summed up as lightless, a Mammoth Cave kind of dark.

Enter Jesus. The fulfillment of the prophet Isaiah's prediction above.

The absence of light met the absence of darkness. "God is light, and in him is no darkness at all" (1 John 1:5). Evil met righteousness. Sin went toe to toe with perfection.

And every time, without exception, where light is introduced even in small proportions, light wins! "The light shines in the darkness, and the darkness has not overcome it" (John 1:5).

That is why the second half of Ephesians 5:8 says, "But now you are light in the Lord. Walk as children of light."

The grand exchange is on. I trade absence for presence. I swap stumbling blindness for illuminated travel. Mammoth Cave for a mountaintop midday.

> *"I am the light of the world."—Jesus*
>
> (JOHN 8:12)

> *"You are the light of the world."—Jesus*
>
> (MATTHEW 5:14)

Do you get the picture? Jesus, the pure light, now in the heart and life of His followers so that we may be "blameless and innocent, children of God without blemish in the midst of a crooked and twisted generation, among whom you shine as lights in the world" (Philippians 2:15).

God is light. Jesus is the light of the world. We are His light in our world. And without stuttering God declares: "Light wins!"

To the glory of God. This is how, and this is why.

A WINNABLE WAR

Finally, be strong in the Lord and in the strength of his might. Put on the whole armor of God, that you may be able to stand against the schemes of the devil. For we do not wrestle against flesh and blood, but against the rulers, against the authorities, against the cosmic powers over this present darkness, against the spiritual forces of evil in the heavenly places. Therefore take up the whole armor of God, that you may be able to withstand in the evil day, and having done all, to stand firm.

(EPHESIANS 6:10-13)

THERE IS AN ENEMY of our soul. He's not passive. He's clever. He's destructive.

He employs cosmic power and devious schemes. He measures his success by the residue, despair, and debris that he leaves in his wake. He uses, abuses, lies, and cheats to accomplish his purposes.

He is real. He is tenacious.

But, he is powerless to stand against the might of the one true God. His weapons turn impotent, his schemes shrivel, his darkness is exposed.

Make no mistake; grace and mercy stand on the reclaimed soil that blood bought. This is war. Every good, every hint of decency, every sacrifice of love, every act of mercy has its genesis in the breath of a gracious God our Father.

"Finally, be strong." The armor left in our closet, the weapons allowed to rust, the strategy that's been relegated to a family room bookshelf exposes vulnerability. It creates opportunity . . . for evil, for the unthinkable.

Every weapon God has issued will be required.

Learn how to apply them. You'll need them throughout your life. God's Word is an indispensable weapon. In the same way, prayer is essential in this ongoing warfare. Pray hard and long. Pray for your brothers and sisters. Keep your eyes open. Keep each other's spirits up so that no one falls behind or drops out.

(EPHESIANS 6:17, 18 MSG)

Make no mistake . . . the battle of good and evil is real, it's demanding, and it's absolutely winnable.

"Having done all . . . stand firm."

No Boilerplate
Answers

He was in the beginning with God. All things were made through him,
and without him was not any thing made that was made.

(John 1:2, 3)

WHAT WAS JESUS LIKE? What terms or characteristics capture His essence?

My journey through the four Gospels has ushered in a fresh perspective and a growing appreciation for the breadth of character and skill. Yes, Jesus is holy, just, forgiving, powerful, loving, compassionate, faithful, true, majestic, and righteous. He also is and was amazingly creative.

Would "creative" have been part of your description of Jesus? How about your description of God? Yet Genesis 1:1 describes a creative process that launched the history of mankind.

Jesus' ministry on earth was laced with creativity. Inspiration bred application in appropriate, unique, and thoughtful ways. This model of living captivates and empowers; at the same time, it shatters a routine, systematic, and uniform engagement with our culture. Jesus never used a checklist for ministry.

To an old man He invited the concept of being born again.

To a dry and thirsty soul He offered living water.

To a crowd hungry for truth He became the bread of life.

For a dark and depraved generation He illuminated.

For bland religion He offered salt.

To the slave He offered freedom.

To the outcast He offered connection.

To the leper He offered touch—His own against neglected and despised skin.

To the condemned He offered grace.

To the disposed He offered justice.

For the sinner He offered salvation.

For the self-absorbed and greedy He offered precise and profound judgment.

To the wanderer He offered a shepherd.

To the fatherless He gave a legacy, an inheritance, a genealogy.

For the orphan He offered an embrace, a lap, a place of honor.

Boilerplate answers didn't apply. Stock solutions were flipped over at the entrance to the synagogue. Jesus invited us to live by the Spirit, in the Spirit, and with the Spirit in concert with His Word.

To a four-year-old girl named Zion whom I sat next to on a flight, He is a listening ear. To a "twentysomething" seatmate dressed from head to toe in black, He is a conversation, an intruder through an artificial barrier.

Always and forever the Good News . . . with context. He is the I Am. Forever the same. Unchanging. But He is, in the moment . . . always aware . . . always God with us. Immanuel.

I'm learning. I'm listening. I'm falling more deeply in love with Jesus.

CARRY IT
TOGETHER

Therefore, confess your sins to one another and pray for one another, that you may be healed. The prayer of a righteous person has great power as it is working.

(JAMES 5:16)

AFTER HELPING OUR SON, Erik, and his wife, Kendal, move into their home one week, I am convinced that armoire is a French word meaning: "piece of furniture so large that no single human being could ever move it." Attractive, functional, but huge.

Erik and Kendal had found this used piece of furniture through Craigslist, and had done a masterful job of refinishing it. They were thrilled with the spot it would occupy in their home. But we all dreaded the prospect of moving it.

So one Saturday, after several hours of avoiding the inevitable . . . it was time. Frankly, and to my surprise, the task proved to be quite manageable with three of us committed and involved.

Several days later, while walking through a hallway in our office, I ran into Linda and Kathy. They're two people who pray. For me. For us. For the mission.

They asked crisp questions about the status of my week, and then assured me that they were praying. The interaction was just a few minutes, but the impact was powerful. A load shared. Burdens distributed. I had help in lifting my personal armoire.

Prayer does that. The suffocated effect of carrying a load alone isn't practical or biblical.

You don't have to go it alone. Pray and be prayed for. Under the beautiful banner of God's love we revel.

No armoire is too large for a community. When we pray, we grab a corner, we lift a load, we share what was never intended to be carried alone.

I know . . . I need . . . I am inspired . . . by praying friends.

AMAZING GOD

And they sing the song of Moses, the servant of God, and the song of the Lamb, saying,
"Great and amazing are your deeds, O Lord God the Almighty!
Just and true are your ways, O King of the nations!"

(REVELATION 15:3)

AT PRECISELY 10:45 ONE morning, I was amazed by something that happened. It's not particularly important what exactly amazed me . . . just that God, in His own, unmistakable and unpredictable way, broke through my routine and interrupted my expectations with something well beyond my ability to ask or comprehend.

God is incredible.

Unconventional. Unhurried. God.

To the extent that He does what I expect, in the time frame that I expect it . . . He ceases to be God.

A burning bush.

A jabbering donkey.

An unexplainable rainstorm.

A large and hungry fish.

An infant king. A controversial life. A brutal death.

Tongues of fire.

Mercy for the guilty.

Our God is astounding.

And in the middle of a scripted day God did what only God could do. He broke through. Arresting my spirit, assaulting my assumptions.

I will never exhaust His vast resources . . . never explain His infinite power . . . never understand His perfect timing . . . never extinguish His powerful love.

At 10:45 . . .

Amazing God.

ABOUT
DAN WOLGEMUTH

DANIEL S. WOLGEMUTH CURRENTLY serves as the ninth President of Youth for Christ/USA.

Dan was raised in Wheaton, Illinois, and is a graduate of Taylor University, Upland, Indiana.

Dan and his wife, Mary, have a long and rich history with the Youth for Christ organization that helped to foster their love for the mission of YFC. Dan's father, Sam, served as President of Youth for Christ/USA from 1965–1973. Dan has served on the National Board of Trustees from 1995 to present. In addition, Dan has served as a volunteer with YFC in Fort Wayne, Indiana and Nashville, Tennessee.

Prior to joining Youth for Christ, Dan worked in a variety of roles for several corporations. Most recently as Senior Vice President and Chief Information Officer for HNTB Companies, Kansas City, Missouri, which is a prominent national engineering and architectural consulting firm. He also served as Vice President and CIO at General Electric, Overland Park, Kansas for eight years.

Dan serves on the Board of Trustees of Taylor University and is a member at Colorado Community Church in Denver.

Dan has written and spoken extensively, and sends a weekly email devotional titled, "Friday Fragments," to over three thousand recipients. He is also the author of *The Monday Memo.Com* (2000).

203

FRAGMENTS

Dan and Mary have been married for over thirty years and have three married children and are the proud grandparents of four grandchildren who all live in the Denver area.

YOUTH FOR CHRIST'S WEBSITE:

www.yfc.org

To sign up to receive Dan Wolgemuth's *Friday Fragments* by email, please contact June Thompson, jthompson@yfc.net

An archive of past *Friday Fragments* is available at www.yfc.org/fragments

ABOUT
YOUTH FOR CHRIST

YFC REACHES YOUNG PEOPLE everywhere, working together with the local church and other likeminded partners to raise up life-long followers of Jesus who lead by their godliness in lifestyle, devotion to the Word of God and prayer, passion for sharing the love of Christ and commitment to social involvement.

Every day at thousands of community centers, high schools, middle schools, juvenile institutions, coffee shops and local hangouts, YFC staff and volunteers meet with young people who need Jesus. Our passion is to see God redeem their stories as we enter into their lives as true friends and mentors. We focus on reaching every young person one at a time.

We are a national movement of adults who engage all sorts of teenagers in caring, supportive and empowering relationships.

We love them . . . we surround them in prayer . . . we explore the Bible with them. Ultimately, we hope to acquaint them with Jesus Christ and journey with them as their lives are changed by God. And we will partner with anyone who can help us make a difference with young people, especially kids who are walking life's desperate edges.